HOW TO MASTER E

**In this Series**

How to Apply for a Job
How to Apply to an Industrial Tribunal
How to Be a Freelance Secretary
How to Be a Local Councillor
How to Be an Effective School Governor
How to Become an Au Pair
How to Buy & Run a Shop
How to Buy & Run a Small Hotel
How to Choose a Private School
How to Claim State Benefits
How to Communicate at Work
How to Conduct Staff Appraisals
How to Counsel People at Work
How to Do Voluntary Work Abroad
How to Do Your Own Advertising
How to Emigrate
How to Employ & Manage Staff
How to Enjoy Retirement
How to Find Temporary Work Abroad
How to Get a Job Abroad
How to Get a Job in America
How to Get a Job in Australia
How to Get a Job in Europe
How to Get a Job in France
How to Get a Job in Germany
How to Get a Job in Hotels & Catering
How to Get a Job in Travel & Tourism
How to Get Into Films & TV
How to Get into Radio
How to Get That Job
How to Help Your Child at School
How to Invest in Stocks & Shares
How to Keep Business Accounts
How to Know Your Rights at Work
How to Know Your Rights: Students
How to Know Your Rights: Teachers
How to Live & Work in America
How to Live & Work in Australia
How to Live & Work in Belgium
How to Live & Work in France
How to Live & Work in Germany
How to Live & Work in Hong Kong
How to Live & Work in Italy
How to Live & Work in Japan
How to Live & Work in New Zealand
How to Live & Work in Portugal
How to Live & Work in Saudi Arabia
How to Live & Work in Spain
How to Lose Weight & Keep Fit
How to Make a Wedding Speech
How to Manage a Sales Team
How to Manage Budgets & Cash Flows
How to Manage Computers at Work
How to Manage People at Work
How to Manage Your Career
How to Master Book-Keeping
How to Master Business English
How to Master GCSE Accounts
How to Master Languages
How to Master Public Speaking
How to Pass Exams Without Anxiety
How to Pass That Interview
How to Plan a Wedding
How to Prepare Your Child for School
How to Publish a Book
How to Publish a Newsletter
How to Raise Business Finance
How to Raise Funds & Sponsorship
How to Rent & Buy Property in France
How to Rent & Buy Property in Italy
How to Retire Abroad
How to Return to Work
How to Run a Local Campaign
How to Run a Voluntary Group
How to Sell Your Business
How to Spend a Year Abroad
How to Start a Business from Home
How to Start a New Career
How to Study Abroad
How to Study & Learn
How to Study & Live in Britain
How to Survive at College
How to Survive Divorce
How to Take Care of Your Heart
How to Teach Abroad
How to Travel Round the World
How to Understand Finance at Work
How to Use a Library
How to Work from Home
How to Work in an Office
How to Work with Dogs
How to Write a Press Release
How to Write a Report
How to Write an Assignment
How to Write an Essay
How to Write Business Letters
How to Write for Publication
How to Write for Television

*Other titles in preparation*

How To...

# MASTER BUSINESS ENGLISH

Michael Bennie

*Second Edition*

'...It's mainly copies of last year's interdepartmental memos.'

**How To Books**

By the same author in this Series

*How to Do Your Own Advertising*

**British Library Cataloguing in Publication Data**
A catalogue record for this book is available from the British Library.


Published by How To Books Ltd, Plymbridge House, Estover Road, Plymouth PL6 7PZ, United Kingdom. Tel: Plymouth (01752) 735251/695745. Fax: (01752) 695699. Telex: 45635.

First edition 1991. Second edition (revised and updated) 1994.



Note: The material contained in this book is set out in good faith for general guidance and no liability can be accepted for loss or expense incurred as a result of relying in particular circumstances on statements made in the book. The laws and regulations are complex and liable to change, and readers should check the current position with the relevant authorities before making personal arrangements.

Typeset by PDQ Typesetting, Stoke-on-Trent.
Printed and bound by The Cromwell Press, Broughton Gifford, Melksham, Wiltshire.

# Contents

# List of illustrations

# Preface

Communication is the key to success in any business. Whether you are trying to sell a product, answer a query or complaint from a customer or convince your colleagues to follow a certain course of action, good communication often means the difference between success and failure. Imprecise, clumsy or long-winded business documents will at best give a poor impression of you or your business; at worst they will be misunderstood or ignored. In contrast, clear, precise writing will be enjoyable to read, and is likely to evoke the response you want.

This book is written for everyone who wants to master the skill of good communication in business—from business people to voluntary workers, government officials to managers, as well as business and secretarial students. The aim is to give you a good grounding in writing style, which you can then apply to any situation. It shows what is good and bad style, what you should avoid and why. It does *not* provide a set of model letters for particular situations. You should think about the letters, memos or reports you write, not just copy someone else's models. So although you will find a great many examples of letters and other documents of all kinds in this book, they are just that—examples to illustrate particular points and particular styles, not models to be copied, parrot-fashion.

The book is arranged in such a way as to be easy to use, whether you are reading it from cover to cover or just dipping into it. It starts with a general discussion of business communication, and then goes on to planning, layout, construction and style. There are chapters on grammar, punctuation and spelling but I have put them towards the end. This is not because grammar and punctuation are unimportant—far from it. But I have arranged the book in this way so that you can refer to those chapters if you need to without them getting in the way of the discussion of style and construction. They contain the minimum of theory, and the emphasis is on the practical applications, and on the sort of common mistakes to avoid.

Throughout the book you will find questionnaires and checklists to help you and to enable you to check your progress. The grammar and punctuation chapters contain exercises to help you test your knowledge of these important elements of good writing. Suggested answers to these exercises are given at the back of the book.

As you improve your mastery of good business English, you will find it very satisfying to be able to express yourself clearly and succinctly on paper, and to get your *precise* meaning across to your readers. Not only do you have the satisfaction of a job well done, but you know that there is a greater chance of getting your audience to react in the way you want them to.

## PREFACE TO THE SECOND EDITION

Since the first edition of this book was published, good communication in business has, if anything, grown in importance. More and more employers are recognising the need for their staff to develop their writing skills, and the syllabuses of the expanding range of vocational courses now increasingly include modules on communication.

Language is constantly changing and developing, and usages which were frowned upon only a few years ago are quite acceptable today. This new edition has been revised to take account of that process. In particular, I have incorporated a number of questions and problems raised by a number of students on my courses over the last few years. I am grateful to them for keeping me on my toes, and for sharing my enthusiasm for well-written, clearly expressed prose.

All the characters and organisations in the case studies are purely fictional, and any resemblance to real individuals or organisations is entirely coincidental.

*Michael Bennie*

# 1 Communicating in Business

What is communication? According to the dictionary, it is:

'the process by which information is exchanged'.

Information in this sense, of course, means not just facts; it also means ideas, emotions and impressions. This exchange can take place in a number of ways:

- through the written word
- through the spoken word
- through pictures and diagrams
- through facial expressions, behaviour and posture
- through non-verbal sounds

Let us look at some of these methods of communication.

## VISUAL COMMUNICATION

Photographs, paintings, drawings and diagrams are all important means of communication. In fact, some concepts are almost impossible to convey without the help of visual images. How could you describe colours, for example, without the use of photographs or paintings? And the complexity of, say, a motor car engine, is very much easier to explain with the help of diagrams than by words alone. Moreover, as we will see in Chapter 3, it is often easier to understand figures if they are expressed in a visual form, such as a graph or a chart.

Visual images have their limitations, however.

- They usually need to be accompanied by verbal explanations.

- It is very hard to convey abstract ideas or thoughts visually.

- Visual images are not as precise as words in conveying shades of meaning, and can therefore sometimes be misunderstood.

Visual communication has its place, and life would be much poorer without it. But it lacks one thing—**precision**. And precision is something that is vital in any form of business communication. It is language, either written or spoken (or in the case of the deaf, signed) that fills that gap, that enables you to say just what you mean, and that ensures that your audience understands you.

## USING WRITTEN AND SPOKEN COMMUNICATION

Jane Lee, the Export Manager of John Smith & Sons Ltd, has had a meeting with a prospective agent in South America, Carlos Rodriguez. Figure 1 (page 12) is a transcript of her verbal report on the meeting. As a verbal report, it is fine, but would it work as a piece of written work? Figure 4 shows the sort of report Jane might have *written*. You can see immediately that it is very different from her verbal report. What are the differences?

### Spoken English uses unnecessary words and phrases

When we speak, we generally use more words than we need to. As a piece of spoken English, Jane Lee's report is actually quite concise. But even she introduces unnecessary and generally meaningless phrases such as:

- 'I must say'—which adds nothing to the sense of the report.

- 'Oh, by the way'—meaning 'I forgot to mention'.

- 'really'—which is too vague to add anything to the word it goes with (what is the difference between a good meeting and a really good one?).

These phrases do not matter much in spoken English—indeed they give you an opportunity to gather your thoughts, so they can actually serve a useful purpose. But business writing needs to be as brief as it can be without losing its meaning.

### Spoken English can be vague

Spoken English is generally vaguer than written English. Jane Lee, for example, talks about

- 'a really good meeting'. What does that *mean*? Was it productive? Was it informative? Did she enjoy it? Was he charming? Was the food and wine good? She could mean any one of those things. But which?

- 'all over South America'. In fact, as she indicates in her reply to Peter Morgan's question, she means 'in a number of the major countries of South America', *not* 'all over'.

- 'things like who matters in each country, how they do business there...' etc. This is a roundabout way of saying 'the business climate'.

This vagueness often does not matter when you are speaking, because very often your tone or gesture indicates to your audience what you actually mean, or they can ask you if anything is unclear. But when you are writing, especially when writing business documents, you need to be precise. Since your readers usually cannot ask you to clarify anything that is unclear, they will either make their own interpretations, which may be wrong, or ignore points they do not understand, which may give them an incomplete picture.

### In spoken English you can go back and correct what you have said

When you are speaking, you can stop in midstream and say something like 'Oh, I meant to say...' or 'Sorry, what I should have said was...', if you have forgotten something or if you suddenly realise that you have said the wrong thing. So Jane Lee says:

- 'sorry, I mean...' when she realises that she has said the opposite of what she means.

- 'Oh, by the way, I forgot to mention...' when something occurs to her that should have been said earlier in her report.

When you are writing, you should plan what you want to say, so that you do not have to go back and correct yourself. This sort of afterthought is common in spoken English, but in written form it gives the document a disjointed appearance, making it difficult to follow.

### When speaking you can respond to feedback from your audience

When you are presenting a verbal report or holding a conversation, you can see or hear your audience's reaction to what you are saying; you can then amend your presentation accordingly. You can see four instances of this in Jane's verbal report.

## A MEETING WITH MR RODRIQUEZ – VERSION 1

*Jane Lee:* I must say, I had a really good meeting with Mr Rodriguez. I think he might be the man for us. He seems to know the market very well, and he already does business all over South America.

*Peter Morgan (Managing Director)*: Which countries exactly?

*Jane Lee*: Argentina, Venezuela, Chile, Colombia, Ecuador and Brazil mainly. He knows the import regulations for the different countries, but I would expect that—we wouldn't be considering him if he didn't! But he also seems to know things like who matters in each country, how they do business there, how we can avoid giving offence without knowing it, any problems there may be about payment, all that kind of thing. He is already agent for quite a few companies—Wilson Fabrics, Richmond Consumer Products, Jackson & Peterson and Simon Black Ltd—but they're all in competition with us, so it doesn't matter—sorry, I mean *none of them* is in competition with us! It does show, though, that he's got the experience, and that he's trusted by some of the big names in consumer products. And their ranges complement ours rather well. Oh by the way, I forgot to mention that he's based in Argentina, which is our fastest-expanding market in South America, so he'll be in a good position to push that expansion along.

*Sarah Brown (Financial Director)*: This all sounds too good to be true. How much does he want to be paid—will he accept our usual commission?

*Jane Lee*: I think he might agree to accept our usual terms initially, but eventually he will want a rather different deal. As you know, we usually pay our agents a straight percentage—usually 10 per cent—on turnover in their area. He wasn't very happy with that, but he might be persuaded to start on 10 per cent. Then he would want to negotiate his commission on a sliding scale.

*James Robinson (Operations Director)*: Sorry, Jane, you've lost me there. What do you mean 'negotiate his commission on a sliding scale'?

*Jane Lee*: What he wants us to agree to is 10 per cent on turnover up to £100,000, then say 12½ per cent if he gets the turnover above £100,000, rising to perhaps 15 per cent if it gets above £200,000. The details would have to be negotiated, but that's the basis. Now I know what some of you may be thinking—why pay him more than our other agents? Well, maybe we ought to be paying them in the same way. After all, £100,000 is about 1½ times our present turnover, and if he can get it up to that, he *deserves* more. Not only that, we could afford to pay him more. The Commercial Counsellor in Argentina speaks highly of him, so I would like to recommend that we take up references from his other clients, and if they're satisfactory, we offer him our usual agency contract, with a sliding scale of commission.

Figure 1. A verbal report.

- When Peter Morgan asks her which countries Rodriguez does business with, she clarifies her vague 'all over South America' statement.

- In response to Sarah Brown's scepticism about Rodriguez's willingness to accept the company's usual terms, she is quick to point out that he might be persuaded to agree to them initially.

- She explains the concept of a sliding scale of commission more clearly in her response to James Robinson's question.

- She sees from the reaction of some of her audience that they are still not convinced ('Now I know what some of you may be thinking'), so she introduces the point about the increase in turnover.

When writing a report, memo or letter, you cannot see or hear your audience's reaction, so you have to anticipate any possible counter-arguments, objections or misunderstandings and answer them with the document. On the other hand, in a written document you can put you arguments in the way *you* want to, without interruption. *You* are in control.

In the written version of her report, Jane anticipates all of the above points as follows:

- She specifies straight away the countries in which Rodriguez does business.

- She says that there is no other agent as well suited to the company's needs so as to 'soften up' the opposition before introducing the possibly contentious issue of Rodriguez's commission.

- She carefully explains the concept of the sliding scale, so as to avoid any misunderstandings.

- She points out that any increase in commission will only come after a substantial increase in turnover so as to defuse any possible objections to paying Rodriguez the higher rates.

### Spoken English often uses colloquialisms

If Jane had been telling her boss or a colleague about her meeting in a

A MEETING WITH MR RODRIGUEZ – VERSION 2

The restaurant was half-empty as we made our way to our table. Looking around me, I was pleased with my choice. Not so expensive that he might think we had money to burn, but good enough to impress him, and with enough room to give us the privacy we needed.

'Well, Miss Lee,' he said when we had placed our order, 'what can I tell you about myself?' His English was perfect, with a delicious hint of an accent. 'I am a well-established businessman in Buenos Aires, with interests in a number of consumer products. I would like to represent you because your range complements what I already handle. I do business in most of the countries of South America, and I represent four major British companies. So, I am big enough to offer the facilities you need, but small enough to give you a personal service.' He smiled a self-deprecating smile, and his face lit up. I could get to enjoy working with this man.

'And you don't mind blowing your own trumpet,' I responded, with an answering smile to take the sting out of the words.

He grinned. 'I'm not blowing my own trumpet,' he protested, 'just giving you the truth.'

'What countries exactly,' I asked. 'And what companies?'

'Argentina, of course, Venezuela, Chile, Colombia, Ecuador and Brazil.' He paused while the waiter poured the wine—a Mouton Cadet—and took a sip. 'Your choice is excellent,' he said. 'And in answer to your second question, Wilson Fabrics, Richmond Consumer Products, Jackson & Peterson and Simon Black Ltd. They will all give me references, I am sure. I can't quote their sales figures, you understand, but I have increased each company's turnover in the area by at least 25 per cent in the last year. Knowing your standing in South America, I believe I could do considerably better for you. 'Now,' he added with that smile of his, 'I am blowing my own trumpet!'

'You know how we stand in South America?'

'Of course. It is my business of know about the markets I serve—who is important, what you need to do to get things done, how to cope with each country's regulations—and which foreign companies are not doing too well.' That hurt, but he was right. South America was anything but a boom market for us.

'Tell me about these things, then,' I countered, to cover my embarrassment. And he did. Anecdotes about other businessmen, stories about politicians and bureaucrats he called by their first names, and marketing strategies that would not be countenanced at the London Business School, but which seemed to work in his territory. By the time the dessert arrived—Raspberry Pavlova for him and a rather special fruit salad for me—I was convinced that he really did know the market inside out.

Figure 2. An example of literary writing.

fairly casual way, she would probably have littered her conversation with slang and colloquialisms. Such expressions are perfectly acceptable in conversation, but look wrong in written work. Even in the more formal situation of a verbal report to the Board, she uses the odd colloquialism, such as:

- 'he might be the man for us'.
- 'all that kind of thing'.

Colloquialisms should not be used in business documents. They look lazy, and they seldom have the precision of meaning that is needed in business.

All these differences can be summed up in the first rule of business writing:

- **Business writing must be clear and precise.**

## SEPARATING BUSINESS AND LITERARY STYLES

We have seen the differences between written and spoken English. But not all writing styles are the same; a style that suits one form of writing might be totally wrong for another. The way you write, even the language you use, will be very different if you are writing a novel, say, from the style you would adopt for a business report. Let us stay with Jane Lee and her meeting with Carlos Rodriguez. Figure 2 shows how she might have described it in a work of literature. What differences can you find between this and the business report shown in figure 4?

### Literary writing is descriptive

The literary account of Jane's meeting contains a great deal of description. The aim is to create atmosphere, and this is often best done by describing such things as the surroundings and the people involved in the story. So we have passages like:

- 'The restaurant was half-empty.'
- 'His English was perfect, with a delicious hint of an accent.'

This kind of description is out of place in business writing. Your readers do not have time to read descriptions which in a business context are no more than background. They want facts. And where description is necessary, it should be factual and objective, not flowery and subjective.

### Literary writing uses direct speech

Throughout the literary description of Jane's meeting, she describes what she and Rodriguez said in the exact words they used—direct speech. This helps to involve the reader, and makes him or her identify with the story. But you would very seldom use direct speech in business writing—it is just too long-winded. Once again, people want to absorb the information you are giving them as quickly and easily as possible. So give them the gist of what was said, not the actual words.

### Literary writing introduces personal feelings

Throughout the literary version, Jane introduces her own feelings about Rodriguez, and about how the meeting is going. She says, for example:

- 'I could get to enjoy working with this man.'
- 'That hurt, but he was right.'

Personal feelings have no place in business writing. Your opinions might be important, depending on the sort of thing you are writing, but your feelings seldom are. They clutter the document unnecessarily.

This brings us to the second rule of business writing:

- **Business writing must be brief and uncluttered.**

## BUSINESS AND PERSONAL CORRESPONDENCE

Business correspondence today is less formal and more conversational than it used to be. Many people think that the style of business letters is very little different from that of personal letters. This is not true. Let us pretend that Jane Lee has written to a friend about her meeting with Carlos Rodriguez, and compare her letter (figure 3) with the business report in figure 4.

There are some similarities between this personal letter and both the verbal report and the work of literature. Like the verbal report, the personal letter introduces colloquialisms ('I stuck to my guns'), and like the work of literature, it introduces personal feelings ('I could find it easy to work with him'). But there are other differences between personal and business correspondence.

**Personal correspondence is subjective**

When Jane writes to her friend, she is writing about what *she* has been doing. That is the main reason for writing. So her letter is naturally concerned with what she did, what she felt, how she reacted. The word 'I' crops up throughout the letter. For example:

- 'I could find it very easy to work with him.'
- 'I stuck to my guns...'
- 'I was really rather pleased...'

Business correspondence should be more objective—the only relevance your actions or feelings have is their impact on your business and the person you are addressing.

**Business correspondence is not read for pleasure**

When we write personal letters, our aim is often to give pleasure to the recipient. So we might introduce funny or interesting anecdotes or stories to liven up the letter. Jane, for example, tells one of Carlos's stories.

In business correspondence, you should not try to entertain or amuse your reader. People read business documents to obtain information as quickly and in as easily digestible a form as possible. They read other things for amusement. So don't tell your favourite story, even if it *does* seem to fit in with the subject.

**Personal letters sometimes exaggerate or use euphemisms**

It is not uncommon to find statements in personal letters which stretch the truth a little in order to show the writer in a good light, or perhaps to spare the feelings of the recipient. Most of us do it at some time. You might say 'I have left my job', rather than 'I have been made redundant', or 'You seemed to get on well with John and Marian at the sales conference', rather than 'You offended the other 52 people there.'

Jane is guilty of this. She says that Rodriguez agreed to accept the usual commission 'with a few adjustments', when in fact he only agreed to consider accepting the commission, and the 'adjustments' were quite major.

This brings us to the third rule of business writing:

- **Business writing must be direct and to the point.**

A MEETING WITH MR RODRIGUEZ – VERSION 3

A few days ago I had a very interesting meeting with a rather nice South American called Carlos Rodriguez. He wants to be our agent out there, and I must say, I could find it very easy to work with him. That smile of his! We had a marvellous lunch, and he had some incredible stories. He seems to know everyone who matters in South America.

I think my favourite story was one about the Minister of Mines in Ecuador. Apparently one of Carlos's competitors had bribed the Minister to get some confidential information for him (I think it was to do with tenders for a government contract), so that he would have the edge over Carlos. The Minister saw Carlos at a party, but he was rather drunk, and mistook him for the competitor. So he took Carlos aside, and gave *him* the information!

Of course I didn't let Carlos's charm, or his stories, influence my decision about his suitability as an agent. He would actually make a very good agent, but we had quite a battle over his commission. However, I stuck to my guns, and eventually he agreed to accept our usual commission, with a few adjustments.I was really rather pleased with myself about that, because he is probably worth a lot more. He is agent for some pretty big companies, and I am sure they must be paying him more than we are offering.

Figure 3. An example of a personal letter.

## THE FUNCTIONS OF BUSINESS CORRESPONDENCE

We have seen the differences between business correspondence and other forms of communication, but do we really need to put things in writing at all? In this age of the telephone, computer link and fax, why should we bother to write things down? It is usually simpler and quicker to pick up the phone, or send something down the computer link.

It is true that innovations in the field of communications have reduced the need for written documents, but there are still many times when it is better to have something in writing. Indeed, one technical innovation, the fax, has to some extent brought business writing back into fashion. A few years ago, if you needed a quick answer to a query or complaint, you might have phoned the person concerned. Today, many people would send a fax; it has the same benefit of speed, but the added advantage of leaving you a written record of the communication.

There are four main reasons for wanting to put your communication in writing. They are:

- to retain a permanent record;
- to provide a basis for discussion;
- to clarify a complex subject;
- to send the same message to a number of people.

Let us look at each of these in turn.

### To retain a permanent record

A conversation can be forgotten, misremembered, misunderstood or even deliberately twisted. But if something is in writing (and if it is well written), everyone who reads it will be sure to get the right information. There are many circumstances in which a permanent written record is not only desirable, but essential. Here are a few examples:

- a report which might need to be referred to in the future;
- a memo, like the one in figure 5, which sets out a new procedure, and which should be available for new and existing staff to refer to;
- a letter which constitutes some form of agreement, and which can be used as evidence in a court of law (see figure 6);
- a letter of complaint, or a letter replying to a complaint, both of which may need to be referred to if the dispute cannot easily be resolved. A typical letter of complaint is shown in figure 7. It is important to be specific about the nature of the complaint, so that you can prove whether it has been satisfactorily answered. See Chapter 6 for more on letters of complaint.

In all these cases, and in many others, it is important to have a permanent record of the communication, either for reference or to resolve a dispute or misunderstanding later.

### To provide a basis for discussion

If a certain subject is due to come up for discussion at a meeting shortly, it can be very useful to put together a **discussion document** setting out the facts of the case, and perhaps even giving your own

## MEETING WITH CARLOS RODRIGUEZ, 25 JULY 1994

On 25 July I met Mr Carlos Rodriguez of Carlos Rodriguez Import SA, Buenos Aires, who had expressed an interest in becoming our agent in South America. I found the meeting both informative and productive. The main points we discussed are as follows.

1. *Market Penetration*

He seems to know the South American market well, and he already does business in many of the countries there, in particular Argentina, Venezuela, Chile, Colombia, Ecuador and Brazil. During our discussions, he displayed a sound knowledge of the business climate of each country and the differences between them. He is based in Argentina, which is our fastest-expanding market in that area, so he will be in a strong position to facilitate that expansion.

2. *Existing Agencies*

His existing agencies include Wilson Fabrics, Richmond Consumer Products, Jackson & Peterson and Simon Black Ltd. He is therefore obviously trusted by some of the major companies selling consumer products. The British Commercial Counsellor in Argentina also speaks highly of him. None of his existing clients is in competition with us—indeed their products complement ours.

No other agent has as good a track record as he does in terms of complementary agencies, nor does anyone else suit our products and market as well as he does. He offers us all we need in South America.

3. *Commission*

The commission arrangements he wants are, however, slightly different from our usual ones. We normally pay agents a straight 10 per cent commission on turnover, and although Mr Rodriguez was initially not keen to accept that low a percentage, I believe that he would agree to start at 10 per cent. What he really wants, however, is a rising level of commission, depending on the turnover he generates. The details would have to be negotiated, but the sort of scale he outlined was as follows:

| | |
|---|---|
| up to £100,000 | 10% |
| £100,000 – £200,000 | 12½% |
| over £200,000 | 15% |

The figure of £100,000 represents about 1½ times our present turnover in the area, and I believe that if he does generate that kind of increase, he has a right to ask for a higher commission. Moreover, if we achieve that level of turnover, we will be able to afford to pay him at a higher rate. If he fails to reach £100,000, of course, we will have lost nothing.

We might receive complaints from some of our other agents if they were to learn that we were paying Mr Rodriguez at a higher level, and it would be worth considering giving all our agents a similar incentive.

4. *Recommendation*

For the moment, whatever we might decide about our other agents in the future, I strongly recommend that we accept the principle of what Mr Rodriguez is asking, take up references from his existing clients and, assuming they are satisfactory, offer him a contract.

Figure 4. A written report.

views and arguments. This saves time at the meeting; instead of having to relate all the facts, you can go straight on to discussing the implications, hearing people's opinions and reaching decisions. It also gives people time to study the facts, so that they come to the meeting prepared to give their views.

A discussion document of this sort can be anything from a 50 page report to a brief memo or letter, depending on the subject and its complexity. The written report by Jane Lee (figure 4), for example, would no doubt form the basis for a discussion by the Board on whether to employ Carlos Rodriguez as their South American agent. If she circulated the report to all Board members in advance, Jane would not have to waste time giving a verbal account at the meeting itself; the discussion would simply revolve around the advantages and disadvantages of doing as she recommended.

### To clarify a complex subject

Some subjects do not lend themselves easily to spoken communication. Let us say, for example, that you want to show that over the last few years your peak sales period has gradually shifted from February/March to April/May (perhaps in order to suggest changes in your production schedule). You could sit across the table from your colleagues, quoting a string of figures at them, but it is unlikely that any of them would absorb them or grasp their significance. On the other hand, a memo setting out the figures in graphic form, as in figure 8 for example, and pointing out the significance of the trend, would have an immediate impact. For more on graphs and charts, see Chapter 3.

Even if you do not have a lot of figures to present, there are subjects which are better shown in a written form, simply because they are too difficult to absorb all in one 'bite'. Look at the letter in figure 9. It would be hard for Peter Richardson to explain the intricacies of his correspondence with his insurers over the phone, but when it is laid out in the way it is, it is immediately clear that there has been considerable confusion on the part of the insurance company.

### To send the same message to a number of people

It will often be quicker, and usually cheaper, to send memos or letters if you want to get the same message across to a number of people. A simple example is the memo in figure 10. You could, of course, have phoned each head of department and told them about the meeting. But by sending a memo, you have saved yourself several phone calls, and you can be sure that each individual knows exactly when and where the meeting is, and what you want to discuss.

To: All Sales Reps
From: David Jones, Sales Manager
21 July 1994

As many of you are only too well aware, we are receiving an increasing number of customer complaints about incorrect deliveries. The reason for this seems to be that order input staff are having difficulty reading their copies of your orders, and so are inputting the wrong items. The problem basically is that they get the bottom copy from your order pad, which is often very faint.

I have therefore decided to change the system. Instead of giving the top copy of the order to the customer, keeping the second copy and sending the third copy to order input, would you in future please send the *top* copy to order input, give the second to the customer and keep the third yourselves. In this way, if anyone has difficulty reading the item it will be you, but since you seldom need to refer to your orders, it will hardly matter.

Figure 5. A memo setting out a new procedure.

Similarly, if your company moves, it is time-consuming and expensive to phone all your customers and suppliers to inform them. It is much easier to do a standard letter like the one in figure 11 and mail it to them. Sales letters, discussed in Chapter 6, are another example of sending the same message to a number of different people.

## CHECKLIST

- Can you recognise the differences between written and spoken English?
- Why is a literary style of writing unsuited to business?
- Why would you not write a business letter like a personal letter?
- What are the four main functions of business correspondence?
- Can you recognise situations in your own experience to which they would apply?

**SPRINGVALE OFFICE SUPPLIES LTD**
Unit 5, Jupiter Business Park, Springvale
Tel (01234) 67535 Fax (01234) 75365

Mr James Potts
Spartan Sports Ltd
23 High Street
Merriton

27 August 1994

Dear Mr Potts

Thank you for your letter of 25 August enquiring about our range of products and our terms.

I am pleased to enclose our latest catalogue, which illustrates and describes all the items we hold in stock. Prices are as shown on the enclosed price list. We guarantee to supply any item within two days of receipt of order.

Our payment terms are thirty days from delivery, and we offer a 10 per cent discount on orders over 200. I look forward to receiving your order.

Yours sincerely

Stephen Benson
Sales Manager

Figure 6. An example of a letter which could be used as evidence of an agreement. Once the customer placed his order, he would be deemed to have accepted Springvale's terms.

THOMAS KINGSTON FOODS LTD

7 Potterton Way
Bramley
Scotland
Tel 567097

2 May 1994

Ms Sarah Walton
Sales Manager
Malvern Fruit Wholesalers
3 Burns Road
Corton

Dear Sarah

I feel I must bring to your attention the fact that your latest shipment of apples (in response to our order 14573) is not up to the standard we have come to expect from you. Many of them are bruised, and more than half were covered in unsightly blemishes. They are classed as Grade A, as per our order, but I think there must have been some mistake, as they are definitely not Grade A apples.

We have always been extremely satisfied with the quality of your produce, which makes this case all the more puzzling. I would be grateful if you would look into the matter. We would be happy to keep the apples and try to sell them at a reduced price, but in that case we would obviously need a credit from you. Alternatively, you could collect them and replace them with apples of the right quality. Perhaps you could phone me to let me know how you want to handle it.

Yours sincerely

Fiona Stockton
Purchasing Manager

Figure 7. An example of a letter of complaint.

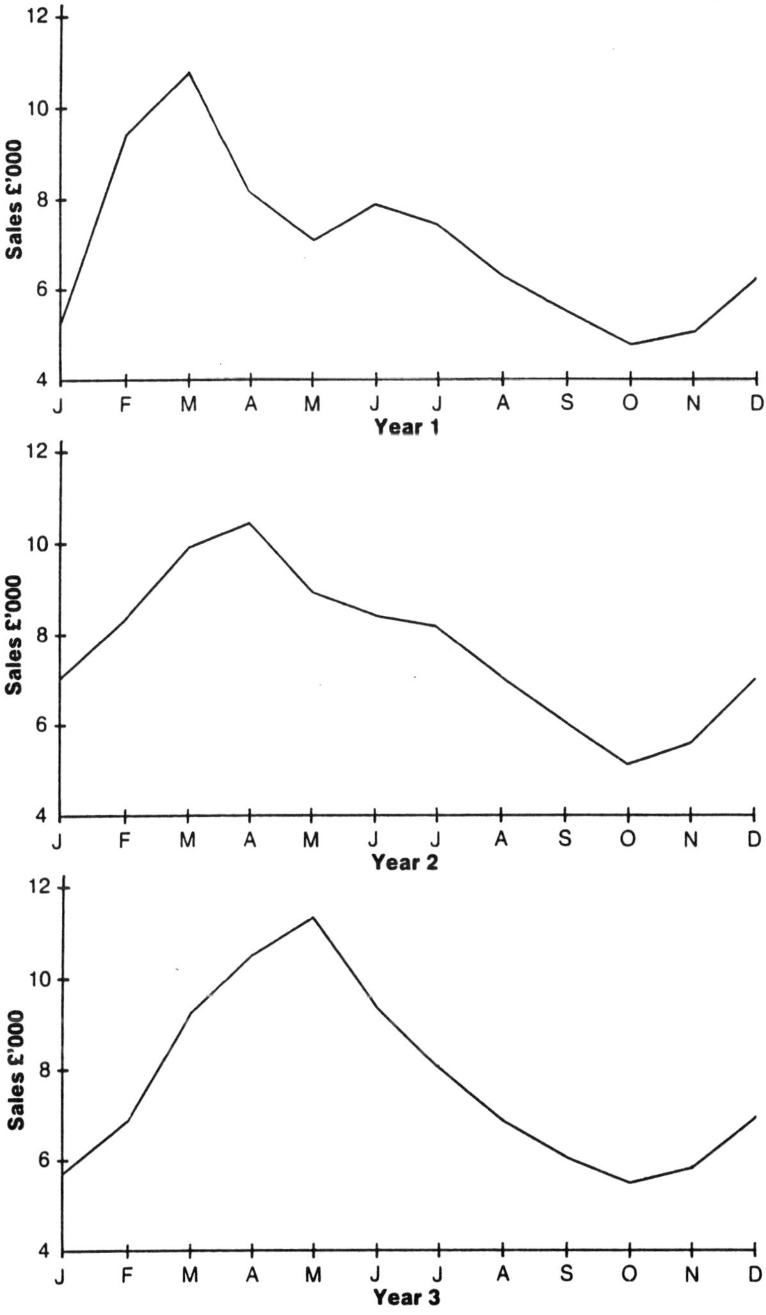


Figure 8. Graphs illustrating trends in sales.

# PETER RICHARDSON

*Building Contractor*

Mr David Carson
Manager
Motorsure Insurance Ltd
2 City Street
Stanton
ST1 3CD

13 Kitchener Street
Morganstown
MT5 6AB
Tel. 567345

12 March 1995

Dear Mr Carson

Policy No 123 4567890

Five months ago, I wrote to you with a simple query regarding the insurance on my van. Since then I have had considerable correspondence with your company, but the position has become no clearer. The situation is as follows:

7 November: I wrote to you, informing you that I had changed my van. You sent me a request for an additional premium.
24 November: I wrote asking why I was required to pay an additional premium, since my new van was the same size and make as the old one, just a newer model. I received no reply.
29 December: I wrote again, explaining the position, and asking for an acknowledgement of my change of van.
7 January: I received a postcard to say that the matter was receiving attention.
27 January: I telephoned your office and spoke to a Mr Jones. He promised to look into the problem. As a result of this phone call, I received a temporary cover note—no letter of explanation, just a cover note with a compliments slip.
1 February: I wrote to Mr Jones asking why he had sent me a cover note when all I needed was a letter confirming that my change of van has been noted and that no additional premium was required.
7 February: I received a letter signed, not by Mr Jones but by a Mrs Kenton, saying that the extra premium demanded was because I now had two vans.
9 February: I wrote to Mrs Kenton pointing out that I did not have two vans. I merely traded my first van in for a newer model.
12 February: I received a form letter from your office (reference FD7/123 456890), informing me that if I did not pay the extra premium within one week, my policy would be null and void.
13 February: I wrote immediately to your Customer Services Manager, outlining the correspondence so far, and asking for some explanation.
18 February: I received a letter from you personally, saying that you had asked for my file to be passed to you, and would be in touch shortly. You enclosed an application form for a new policy, although I cannot understand why. I have not heard from you since.

..../

I now do not know where I stand. Am I still insured with you? Am I insured for one van or two? Am I insured for my old van (which I no longer own) or my new one? The position is that I possess one van, a Ford Escort, registration number K123 ABC. Please will you confirm that I am covered for that vehicle, and that vehicle only, and that I am not required to pay any additional premium.

I am sure you will appreciate that this uncertainty is affecting my business. In order to protect myself, therefore, I will have to pass copies of our correspondence to your trade association unless I hear from you within the next three days.

Yours sincerely

Peter Richardson

Figure 9. A letter clarifying a complex issue.

To: All Department Heads
From: James Grant 19 September
1994

There will be a meeting of all heads of department in the boardroom on Monday, 24 September, to discuss the reorganisation of office accommodation. Please could you all bring your copies of the new office plan, together with your ideas on how you plan to use the accommodation allocated to you.

Figure 10. A memo notifying a number of people of a meeting.

**JOHN BROWN DIY SUPPLIES**

25 King Street, Compton, Larkshire
Tel. (01890) 12345

To all our customers and suppliers 21 February 1995

We are delighted to tell you that we are moving to larger and more central premises, with easier access and more parking. We will therefore be in an even better position to serve our customers, and to handle deliveries from our suppliers.

As from 1 March, our address will be: 27 Union Street, Compton. Our telephone number remains the same.
Yours sincerely

John Martin
Proprietor

Figure 11. A standard letter announcing a change of address.

# JAMES LONG & CO

*FURNITURE MANUFACTURERS AND SUPPLIERS*

125 Broadlands Road
Valley Industrial Estate
Storton ST3 4AB
Tel: 1234567

12 December 1994

Mrs J. Brown
Cliff Hotel
Marine Drive
Oldport

Dear Mrs Brown

I was very sorry to hear from your letter of 3 December that the legs of one of the occasional tables supplied to you recently are coming off.

I have undertaken a thorough investigation of the problem, and I have discovered what went wrong. It appears that a batch of the fixing brackets we use for that particular range was faulty. Our quality control procedures picked up the fault soon after we took delivery, and that batch was put to one side for return to the manufacturer.

Unfortunately, we have recently taken on a new member of staff, and he mistook the faulty brackets for the batch that had been laid out for him to use. Our quality control procedures at the end of the production process are only designed to find faults in our own workmanship, assuming that the pre-production checks will have picked up faults in bought-in components.

As a result of your letter I have changed our procedures, and we now check all our finished products for faults both in our own workmanship and in bought-in components. We now also ensure that any items to be returned to our suppliers are kept well away from the production line.

Yours sincerely

Donald Benson
Production Manager

Figure 12. A letter written without bearing in mind its purpose.

# 2
# Effective Planning

Whatever you are writing, it is important to plan your document. You need not spend a great deal of time on a very routine letter, but even that will need *some* planning. And if you have a standard letter, such as a standard response to a common enquiry, then you obviously don't need to plan each one individually. But you do need to plan the original standard version, and you do need to think carefully about whether, as it stands, it is the most suitable response to the particular query.

The purpose of planning is to ensure that:

- the document you produce says precisely what you want it to say;
- you say everything that has to be said;
- the information you give is correct;
- your arguments are logically expressed;
- you use the right language to suit your purpose;
- you are not emotional.

It is just possible that you might achieve all of these things without proper planning, but it is highly unlikely, and you would certainly not achieve them every time if you always did your business writing 'cold'.

## YOUR REASONS FOR WRITING

Before you even begin to plan your document, you should ask yourself the following questions:

1. Should you be writing at all, rather than phoning or visiting the person concerned?
2. Are you writing to the right person at the right level in the organisation? It is no use writing to an assistant manager, for example, if it is the manager who will have to make a decision on your letter, or to the production manager about something that is the responsibility of the sales manager.

**JAMES LONG & CO**
*FURNITURE MANUFACTURERS AND SUPPLIERS*
125 Broadlands Road
Valley Industrial Estate
Storton ST3 4AB
Tel: 1234567

12 December 1994

Mrs J. Brown
Cliff Hotel
Marine Drive
Oldport

Dear Mrs Brown

I was very sorry to hear from your letter of 3 December that the legs of one of the occasional tables supplied to you recently are coming off.

I have undertaken a thorough investigation of the problem, and I have discovered what went wrong. I won't bore you with the details. Suffice it to say that a combination of human error and problems with our quality control procedures resulted in a few faulty tables leaving our factory. As a result of your letter, we have changed our procedures to make sure that this sort of mistake is not made again. We will of course be happy to replace any of your tables which are not up to our usual high standards. You only mention one in your letter, but to be on the safe side, I would like to have the whole consignment checked. Could you let me know when it would be convenient for our representative to call? He will then check all your tables, and arrange for any which are faulty to be replaced.

Thank you for drawing this problem to my attention, and please accept my apologies for the inconvenience you have been caused.

Yours sincerely

Donald Benson
Production Manager

Figure 13. How the letter in figure 12 should have been written.

If the answer to both these question is yes, then you should ask yourself two further questions.

3. Should copies go to anyone else? You can plan the most beautiful document, but if you do not send it to everyone who needs to read it, it will not serve its purpose.

4. Do you need a reply? If you do, and the document does not say so, it will have failed to achieve its purpose. (See Chapter 3 for more on how to ensure that your correspondent knows what you expect him or her to do.)

Finally, there are two more questions to ask yourself.

5. What is your purpose in writing?

6. What do you want to achieve?

Let us look at these two in more detail.

**What is your purpose in writing?**

This might seem an unnecessary question. After all, you would not be writing if you did not have a reason. But it is important to clarify in your own mind just what your purpose is, and to bear it in mind as you write your letter, memo or report. Look at the letter in figure 12. Can you see what is wrong with it?

It is quite a good letter, but it is not suitable for the purpose for which it was written. Donald Benson obviously knew why he was writing to Mrs Brown—to answer her complaint. But he did not have that thought clearly in his mind when he planned his letter. The result is that he gives a full explanation of how the problem arose, but does not actually answer her complaint. Mrs Brown is not likely to be interested in the details of how her table came to be faulty. What she wants to know is what the company is going to do about it—and Donald does not tell her.

Only by keeping in mind *why* you are writing to someone can you be sure that what you say is relevant both to the subject matter and to the person you are writing to. What Donald Benson says is relevant to the subject, but not to the person.

So how should he have written? Look at the letter in figure 13. Can you see why this is better suited to its purpose? It keeps the explanation to a minimum, it apologises gracefully, and it offers a remedy. This is more the kind of letter Donald should have written if he had kept his purpose in mind as he planned it.

This is not to say that the sort of detail given in figure 12 is never appropriate. If Donald had been asked by the Managing Director to explain how the table came to be faulty and how he intended to ensure that a similar problem did not occur again, he might have written something like the memo in figure 14. As you can see, it is very similar in content to figure 12. In this case, however, Donald's purpose is to explain to his boss what went wrong with the manufacturing process, so the detail he gives is extremely relevant.

It is easier to plan a piece of writing if it only has one purpose—applying for an agency, for example, or setting up a meeting, or reporting on an investigation. You can concentrate on getting your content, style, tone and wording right for that purpose. But there will be times—usually with letters—when you might have to cover two subjects in the same document. You might need to write to a customer, for example, to explain about a change in distribution arrangements, and also to chase an overdue payment. It would be silly to write two separate letters, so you would cover both subjects in one. The best way to handle this situation is to separate the two subjects, and deal completely with one before introducing the other. There will need to be some device to link the two subjects, but otherwise the two parts of the letter are best planned separately.

You can see how this is done in figure 15. The two subjects are dealt with in two separate sections of the letter, separately planned, and linked with the phrase 'While I am writing'.

### What do you want to achieve?

Do not confuse your purpose with what you want to achieve. The two are related but different. For example, Donald Benson wrote his letter to Mrs Brown (figures 12 and 13) to answer her complaint. That was his purpose. What he wanted to achieve was to satisfy her, and to make her feel better about the company. Your purpose will dictate what goes into your letter, while the outcome you want will dictate the style and tone you use.

Let us look at a few more examples to get this distinction clear.

- The purpose of a sales letter is to tell people about your product or service. What you want to achieve is a sale.
- The purpose of a letter of complaint is to complain. What you want to achieve is the correction of the fault or error, or else compensation.
- The purpose of a credit control letter is to chase an overdue payment. What you want to achieve is a cheque in the post.

To: James Long
From: Donald Benson
12 December 1994

Re: Faulty tables supplied to the Cliff Hotel, Oldport

On 8 December you asked me to investigate a complaint from the above customer regarding occasional tables supplied on 30 November.

I have traced Mrs Brown's order back through the production process and have discovered what went wrong. It appears that a batch of the fixing brackets we use for that particular range was faulty. Quality Control picked up the fault soon after we took delivery, and that batch was put to one side for return to Peter Stevens Ltd, the manufacturers.

We have recently taken on a new member of staff, however, and seeing the box of faulty brackets near his work station, he thought that they were there for him to use. An experienced worker would not have made the same mistake, since they all know that the components laid out for them to use are not kept in the original manufacturers' boxes.

The error was not picked up at the end of the production process, because our quality control procedures at that stage are only designed to find faults in our own workmanship. Our quality controllers assume that the pre-production checks will have picked up faults in bought-in components.

As a result of this problem, I have changed the quality control procedures, and Quality Control now check all our finished products for faults both in our own workmanship and in bought-in components. I have also issued instructions to the effect that any items to be returned to suppliers are to be kept well away from the production line.

Figure 14. A memo explaining the background to a customer's complaint.

- The purpose of a report on the advantages and disadvantages of different work practices is to inform the decision-makers of the options available. What you want to achieve is acceptance of the most efficient option.

**COLOURSCHEME PAINTS LTD**

53 King's Way, Topperton AB23 4CD
Tel. (0123) 98765 Fax. (0123) 43210

12 March 1995

Mr Patrick Swan
Proprietor
The Paint and Paper Shop
4 Queen Street
Winterborough
ST12 3UV

Dear Mr Swan

You will be pleased to know that as from 1 April we will be instituting a new improved distribution system. There are two changes, both of which are intended to provide you with a faster, more efficient service.

The first change is in our own internal systems. We are now able to turn your orders around on the day they are received, so that the goods are ready for despatch the following morning. The second is in our carriers. As from 1 April we will be using XYZ Haulage Ltd, who offer a guaranteed 24-hour delivery service. The combination of these two changes means that you should in future receive delivery of your goods no later than 48 hours after we receive your order.

While I am writing, perhaps I could mention that there is an amount of £156.79 overdue on your account. We do not appear to have received payment of our invoice No 09876 of 20 January. As you know, our terms are 30 days from the date of invoice, so this payment is now well overdue. I would be grateful if you would let me have your cheque for this amount as soon as possible.

Yours sincerely

Michael Milton
Sales Manager

Figure 15. A letter combining details of improved service with a request for payment of an overdue account.

To: Brian Carter, Purchase Ledger Clerk
From: Sandra Jones, Accountant
7 September 1994

The Purchasing Manager has complained to me that he is unable to maintain reasonable stocks of many items because we are constantly being put on stop by one supplier or another. This in turn is having an adverse effect on sales. This complaint has put me in an extremely embarrassing position, as I have been criticising the Sales Department in management meetings for their poor performance.

There is absolutely no excuse for holding up payments, especially to major suppliers. Your instructions are to pay all invoices as soon as they are cleared. This you have clearly failed to do on a number of occasions, and I want to know why, and what you intend to do to ensure that it does not happen again. Please give me a report on the situation by Thursday.

Figure 16. A memo unlikely to achieve the outcome the writer wants.

To: Brian Carter, Purchase Ledger Clerk
From: Sandra Jones, Accountant
7 September 1994

The Purchasing Manager has complained to me that he is unable to maintain reasonable stocks of many items because we are constantly being put on stop by one supplier or another. This in turn is having an adverse effect on sales.

Something is obviously going wrong with our payment system, because as you know we should be paying invoices as soon as they are cleared. The problem may be that they are not being cleared quickly enough, or there may be delays within our department. Either way, I think we need to look at the system to see how we can speed things up.

Could you look into the problem for me, and find out what has gone wrong? I would like to discuss your conclusions, together with any suggestions you have for improving the situation, on Thursday.

Thanks.

Figure 17. A memo more likely to get the recipient's co-operation and achieve its aim.

What do you want to achieve with *your* document? Keep it in mind as you plan and write it. As I have said, the outcome you are looking for will influence the tone and style of what you write. Look at the memo in figure 16. Sandra Jones is quite clear about the purpose of her memo—to get Brian Carter to see why the company is so slow in paying its accounts. But is she as clear about what she wants to achieve and how to achieve it?

What she wants to achieve is to find out why the company is so slow in paying, and to ensure that the process is speeded up so that supplies are no longer stopped. But will this memo achieve that aim? Look at the memo she might have written (figure 17). If you were Brian Carter, which of the two would you prefer to receive? Which would make you more likely to co-operate, and which would simply put you on the defensive?

*Comment: memo 1*

Apart from its obvious rudeness, the first memo is less likely to achieve its aim because:

(a) it makes an accusation, so that Brian is liable to act defensively and look for excuses rather than explanations;

(b) it assumes that the fault lies within Brian's area of responsibility, whereas it might lie with the person who is responsible for clearing the invoices, or with the whole system;

(c) it gives him an order rather than inviting his co-operation, so that his reaction could well be to do just as much as is required to satisfy Sandra and get him out of trouble, and no more.

*Comment: memo 2*

The second memo, on the other hand, will probably achieve her aim, because:

(a) it is not accusatory, so that even if Brian finds that he is at fault, he is unlikely to be afraid to admit it;

(b) it does not allocate blame, so that he is encouraged to look into all the stages an invoice has to go through, resulting in a thorough investigation;

(c) it asks for his help and for his suggestions, so that he, as the person closest to the payment system, is encouraged to come up with recommendations for improving it.

## GETTING THE RIGHT REACTION

### Getting to know your audience

The first step towards achieving the outcome you want is to get to know your audience. The style, the tone, even the content of your communication will depend so much on who will be reading it. There are three main categories of people you might write to, each of which will need to be treated differently:

- people with little knowledge of the business you are in;
- people who know something about the business, but not necessarily about your own particular organisation;
- people who not only know the business in general, but how your particular organisation works.

Which category does your correspondent fall into? A member of the public, for example, will usually fall into the first category, but an agent might fall into either the second or the third, depending on how closely integrated he or she is with your company. The way you write your document, and in particular the language you use, will depend on which of these categories your reader falls into. If you were a publisher, for example, reporting that a book is no longer available, you could do so in any one of the following three ways, but only one would be suitable for the particular person you were writing to.

(a) *Practical Goosekeeping* is now reporting O/P. We are considering either a reprint or a new edition, but we cannot make a decision until we have a pre-production costings and proposal form. In the meantime we are recording dues.

(b) I am afraid that *Practical Goosekeeping* is out of stock at present, although we are considering reprinting it. I shall keep your order on file, and let you know the position as soon as we have made a decision.

(c) I am afraid that *Practical Goosekeeping* is currently out of print. A reprint or new edition is under consideration, and we are therefore recording your order on our dues file.

Which would you use for each of the three categories of correspondent? Example (a) and (c) are obviously too full of jargon for members of the public, who would not know what dues are, nor a pre-production costings and proposal form, and would probably not be too sure of the difference between a reprint and a new edition. So (b) would be best for them.

Booksellers would know something about the business, and be likely to understand 'dues' and 'out of print', 'reprint' and 'new edition'. But they would probably not know the intricacies of the pre-production costings and proposal form. So they should receive version (c). The first version would, of course, make complete sense to your colleagues in the firm.

### Questions to ask yourself

But it is not just a question of categorising your readers according to how much they know about your business. There are other factors to be taken into account if you are to suit your communication to your audience. To help you get a better understanding of the people who will be reading your document, ask yourself the following questions:

1. How intelligent are they? It is better to overestimate people's intelligence slightly than to underestimate it and talk down to them.
2. Do they know anything about the subject matter of the document, or are there ideas or technical terms that will need explaining?
3. What is your relationship with them? Is it formal or informal?
4. Are they expecting to hear from you? If not, will they be interested in what you have to say?
5. What do *they* believe is important? For example, if you are presenting a report suggesting that a company social club be set up, you should not simply say how good it would be for staff morale if the person to whom you are addressing it is more concerned with profit margins than staff morale. You would be better pointing out how cheap it would be to do, and then suggest that the improvement in staff morale could bring an improvement in commitment and productivity.
6. What are they likely to agree to readily, and what will they need to be persuaded about? This will affect the order in which you present your points, and the space you devote to them.

Once you know what your audience is like, keep that in mind as you write. Try to see what you are writing from their point of view. Imagine yourself opening the letter, reading the memo, ploughing through the report. How would *you* feel about reading it ?

SQUIRES AND CORNISH
*Financial Consultants*
3 The Square
Marchester
MA1 9YZ
Tel: (01345) 67890 Fax (01345) 12345

1 February 1995

Ms Marian Matthews
Alpha Insurance plc
4 King Street
London EC1 5XY

Dear Ms. Matthews

I would like to apply to act as an agent for Alpha Insurance in this area. We are a small partnership with a substantial volume of business in the insurance, mortgage and financial consultancy fields. Indeed, I believe that we have the largest clientele of any independent financial consultants in Marchester. We are, of course, a FIMBRA member.

We are hoping to expand even more, and could well take on more partners in the near future. In looking for new agencies, we were very interested to see the variety of services you offer, and I am sure that many of our clients would benefit from your range. I also notice that you do not appear to have an agency in the Marchester area.

I would be grateful if you would consider our request and let me know your terms. I would be happy to travel to London to meet you, and I can of course provide suitable references should you decide that you would like to take the matter further.

Yours sincerely

Julia Squires
Senior Partner

Figure 18. A letter written in a formal style.

## Choose the right language

Once you know your audience, you can decide what sort of language you need to use. Should it be technical or non-technical, formal or informal, simple or complex?

**Acme Advertising**
35 Albany Street
Queenstown
QU2 4TX
Tel. (01987) 48723

24 April 1995

James King
Managing Director
Paragon Interiors
4 Brownhill Drive
Queenstown

Dear James

Many thanks for the lunch on Tuesday. It was, as usual, a most enjoyable meal.

I have done a rough costing on the brochure we discussed. I will, of course, send you the formal estimate when our financial people have completed it, but my first reaction is that we should be able to meet your needs within the budget you have set, with one proviso. As I said over lunch, a company like yours needs to project an upmarket image, and that calls for a high-quality production. So rather than producing a 16-page brochure and having to skimp on quality I would suggest doing 8 pages, highly illustrated on quality art paper. Of course, there is another alternative—you could increase your budget!

I will be in touch with the formal estimates shortly, but I felt you might want to know my thoughts before your Board meeting on Monday.

With kind regards
Yours sincerely

Fiona Thompson

Figure 19. A business letter written in an informal style.

The examples given above for a publisher reporting the non-availability of a book show how the degree of 'technicality' can vary according to the audience you are addressing. There are similar variations in the degree of informality you can introduce. Look at the letter in figure 18. This is a formal letter, using formal language, which suits the audience. Julia Squires does not know Marian Matthews and her letter is a formal application for an agency. The sort of approach used in figure 19, for example, would be totally inappropriate.

The language used in figure 19, on the other hand, is quite appropriate for the kind of communication it is—an informal letter to someone Fiona obviously knows well, with whom she has just had lunch, and with whom she enjoys a good business relationship.

So whereas Julia uses expressions like 'indeed', 'I would be grateful' and 'should you decide', Fiona says things like 'many thanks', 'skimp on quality' and 'I felt you might want to know my thoughts'. Simple expressions like these can give a letter a completely different tone.

The nature of your audience will also dictate how simple your language should be. Business English should never be very complex, but you can sometimes introduce fairly complex concepts, if you feel that your audience will understand them. Let us imagine a report on the possibility of developing a new market in an imaginary country. It might include a paragraph like this:

*Example: developing a new market overseas*
There are great risks in trying to open up a market in Sulanesia.

1. It has a monocultural economy. In 1993/4 bananas accounted for 85 per cent of the country's exports and an extremely large proportion of its Gross National Product (the precise percentage cannot be ascertained, as much of the country's economic activity takes place in the informal sector). This leaves it extremely vulnerable to fluctuations in world prices.

2. It is extremely unstable politically. There have been five coups, two coup attempts and one 'palace revolution' in the last ten years, and the present president does not look very secure.

*Comment*
This passage assumes a certain amount of intelligence, and in particular a knowledge of current affairs. Only someone who reads

To: All Directors
From: Alan Walters, Systems Director
3 April 1995

I have been concerned for some time that we are not getting the most out of our computer systems. This is no reflection on the staff in my department, all of whom work extremely hard. It is simply that we do not have the number of properly trained staff we need if we are to serve other departments well.

Departments are currently having to wait up to six months for any new development in their systems. The Production Department, for example, wanted a very minor modification to the program for producing cost prices but had to wait four months, simply because my staff were too busy to make the necessary changes earlier. And when we finally got round to writing the program the Accounts Department wanted for analysing sales and costs by product line, it needed a great deal of debugging, because I had had to allocate it to someone who did not have the right knowledge; Celia Brown, the only person in the department with experience of that kind of work, was involved in another, more urgent, project. And of course the time I had to spend debugging the program could have been better spent on other, more productive, work.

These are just two of the more recent problems caused by the lack of staff, and both of them have, I understand, caused a number of difficulties for the departments concerned, and a loss of efficiency all round.

I therefore think that we should, as a matter of urgency, make a new appointment to the Systems Department, that of Project Leader. He or she would report to the Systems Manager, and would be responsible for new development work. I would like to discuss this at our next meeting.

Figure 20. A memo requesting additional staff.

quite a lot about world affairs would understand concepts such as 'monocultural economy', 'Gross National Product', 'the informal sector' and 'palace revolution'. A report aimed at people who were not quite so well read would have to find other ways of explaining these concepts.

As I have said, however, it is unwise to talk down too obviously to your audience. If you are not sure whether they will understand a particular point, you can get around the difficulty by explaining it, but prefacing your explanation with something like 'As you will know' or 'I am sure you are aware'. In that way, those who are aware will not feel that you are insulting their intelligence, and those who are not still have the concept explained.

Whatever language you decide is appropriate for your audience, there are two things you should *never* do, in any circumstances.

1. **You should never be rude or abrupt**. Even if you are making a complaint, make it politely. Even a final demand for payment can be expressed in courteous terms. Some managers seem to think that memos to their junior colleagues do not matter, and that they can be as rude as they like. This was obviously Sandra Jones's view when she wrote the memo in figure 16. But rudeness like this is not only bad manners. It will not get the reaction you want.

2. **You should never be emotional**. It is important in business documents that you present facts and reasoned arguments, not emotional outbursts. Of course, you may well feel angry about something, but wait until your anger has cooled before you write your letter. Otherwise your emotion is likely to get in the way of your writing, and the finished product will not be as effective in achieving the reaction you want.

### Checking your facts

As we saw in Chapter 1, it is important that a business document should be precise. This precision not only applies to its meaning, but also to its content. Do ensure that your facts are accurate, and that all the necessary facts are provided.

It is sloppy to provide inaccurate information, and it will reflect badly on you. But it can also cause other problems. Look at the memo in figure 20. It is fine as it stands, providing all the information is correct. But let us assume that Alan got his projects confused, and that it was another program that needed all the debugging—the Accounts Department program had only just been completed, so he did not yet know whether it needed debugging or not. People reading the memo who knew that the Accounts Department program had only just been completed (the Financial Director, for example), might well become suspicious of the rest of it. Alan would begin to lose credibility. His reasons for taking on a project leader would still be valid, but he would have more difficulty in convincing the other directors.

Check, too, that you have *all* the relevant facts. You can construct a most convincing argument if you are selective in the information you use, but it can be completely destroyed by someone who has all the facts. Alan Walters's argument in favour of employing a project leader is strong as it stands. But it would be considerably weakened if one of the other directors were to point out that the current rate of new development is a short-term phenomenon, while the company brings its systems up to date. In that case, the Board could quite legitimately argue that a better alternative would be to hire a freelance consultant for a few months to cope with the extra work.

## BEGINNING THE WRITING PROCESS

Now we are ready to start putting something on paper. There are five stages in the planning of your document:

1. First you need to **assemble all your arguments**, so that you can explain yourself or argue your case as effectively as possible.

2. You then need to write an **outline** of what you are going to say.

3. The outline has to be organised into a **logical order**, with the document 'flowing' from one point to the next.

'...It's mainly copies of last year's interdepartmental memos.'

4. Once you have the order sorted out, you are ready to compile your first **draft**.

5. This draft must then be **edited** into the final version.

Of course not all business documents need the same amount of attention. If you were writing a short, fairly simple memo, you would not go through all these processes in detail, although you would be well advised to skip through them mentally, at the very least. On the other hand, if you had a long report to compile, you would be foolish not to spend quite a lot of time on each stage. Now let us look at each of these stages individually.

## Assembling your arguments

Do collect all the information you need before you commit anything to writing. If you are answering a complaint or enquiry, do you have the answers to *all* the points raised? If you are writing a report have you considered *all* the arguments before reaching your conclusion? If you are making an enquiry, do you know *exactly* what you are trying to find out?

When you have all the information you need at your fingertips, you can start marshalling your arguments and the points you want to make. You must present what you want to say in a coherent, logical way, otherwise you will either lose your readers through boredom or misunderstanding, or not make your point effectively. There are two ways of making a convincing point, both equally valid:

- by deduction

- by induction

### *Arguing by deduction*

Deduction involves reasoning from one statement to another to reach a valid conclusion—*deducing* the answer. Let us look at an example. You are involved in the manufacture of furniture, and you are making a case for changing your timber supplier. Your report to your colleagues contains the following:

> Whenever our machines are left idle, we lose money. Continuity of production is vital to our business, and continuity of production depends on a guaranteed supply of raw materials. Our present timber supplier is unable to guarantee supplies of the woods we need, and has let us down on several occasions. We therefore cannot guarantee continuity of production.

In this passage, you make two statements on which your whole argument rests (your **premises**): 'continuity of production depends on a guaranteed supply of raw materials' and 'our present supplier is unable to guarantee supplies'. By a process of deduction, you conclude that 'we cannot guarantee continuity of production'. And if both your premises are true, your readers cannot fault your argument.

But beware of false deductions. Look at the following extract:

> Continuity of production depends on a guaranteed supply of raw materials. The new supplier can guarantee our supplies. With the new supplier, therefore, we will be able to guarantee continuity of production.

This is a false deduction, because guaranteed supply is only *one* of the factors necessary for continuity of production.

You can see the difference between these two arguments if you change the first premise of each to read 'Continuity of production depends, *amongst other things* on a guaranteed supply of raw materials.' In the first argument, the second premise ('The supplier is unable to guarantee supplies') nullifies one of the 'things' on which continuity depends, so the whole continuity is nullified. In the second argument, the second premise ('The supplier *can* guarantee supplies') confirms one of the 'things', *but only one of them*. Unless the others are also confirmed, the continuity cannot be confirmed.

*Arguing by induction*

Induction involves reasoning from your experience, or from your own investigation. Unlike a conclusion arrived at by deduction, a conclusion arrived at by induction cannot usually be proved beyond any doubt. But you should be able to show that:

- the conclusion is reasonable given the information at your disposal;
- your knowledge or experience covers a wide area or sample;
- the sample on which you are basing your conclusion is typical of the circumstances, people, objects, areas etc. of the whole group.

Let us look at an example. You are writing a report on your sales force, and you include the following passage:

> Our sales this year are down by 10 per cent on last year, and I believe that the reason is that the sales force is not working as efficiently as it should. I have examined the records of a sample of ten representatives, and in each case I found deficiencies.

The report would no doubt go on to enumerate the deficiencies you found, but we are only concerned with your argument and your conclusion that the sales force is not working as efficiently as it should. This is an example of argument by induction. You have conducted an investigation and your conclusion is based on the knowledge and information gained during that investigation. Your conclusion cannot be proved beyond any doubt, but it is a valid assumption to make given the results of your investigation.

But it is only a valid assumption if it fulfils the criteria listed above. What if the drop in sales was the result of production difficulties, not a drop in orders—in other words you had the orders but were unable to fulfil them? In this case the conclusion would not be reasonable given the information at your disposal, and your conclusion would not satisfy criterion (a) above. And if there were 40 representatives in your sales force, then the records of only 10 of them would not represent a large enough sample, so you would not satisfy criterion (b). If you had only 20 representatives, then 10 would be a reasonable sample to take. But if you chose as your sample the ones with the worst records, then they would not be typical, and you would not satisfy criterion (c).

Whether you are arguing by deduction or induction, it is very easy to be led into false conclusions, and if your reader picks up the fact that one of your conclusions is false, it will at best weaken your argument, and at worse destroy it.

### Writing an outline

There are three ways of writing an outline. It does not matter which one you use—in fact many people combine techniques. Try them all out and choose whichever suits you best. The three methods are:

- listing
- charting
- freewriting

*Listing*

Probably the most common method is listing. All it involves is making a list of the points you want to make in your document. Do not worry about the order, just list them, one under the other, in the order in which you think of them. But do not try to combine two points on the same line—it only complicates the next step.

Some people use two different coloured pens, and write important points in one colour and others in another. Or they write all the points in one colour and use a highlighter pen to emphasise the important ones. The main thing is to list anything you think might be relevant—

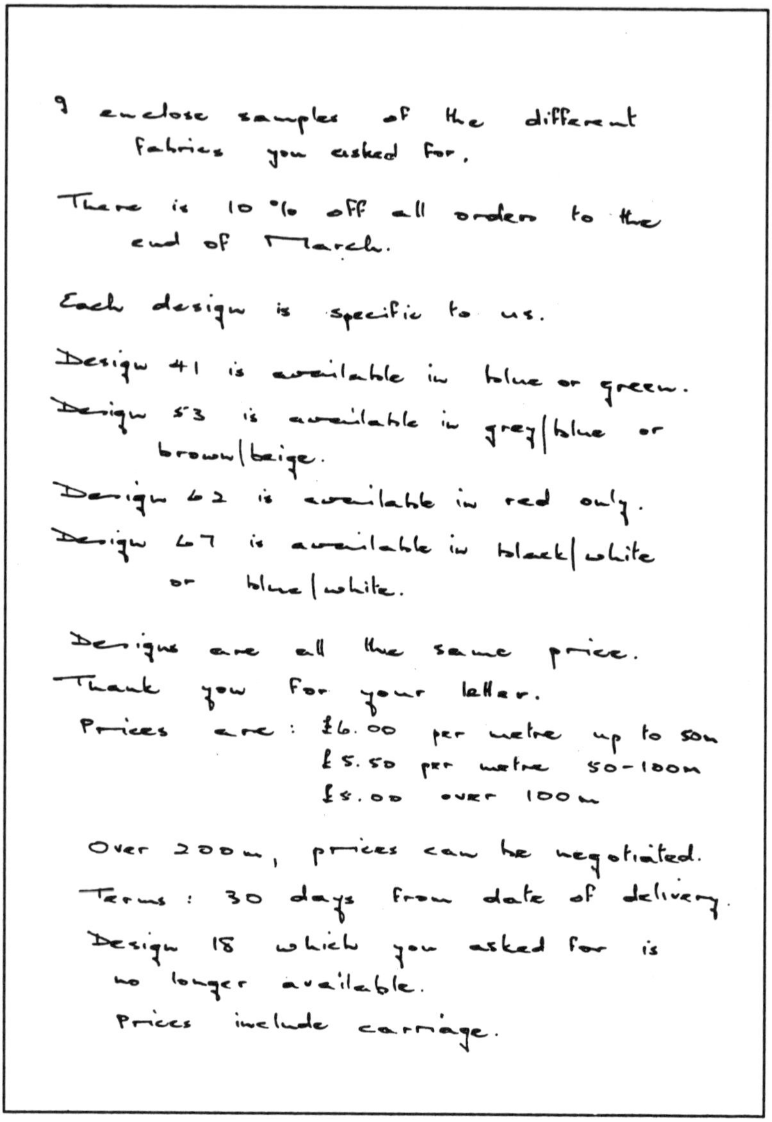
I enclose samples of the different fabrics you asked for.

There is 10 % off all orders to the end of March.

Each design is specific to us.

Design 41 is available in blue or green.

Design 53 is available in grey/blue or brown/beige.

Design 62 is available in red only.

Design 67 is available in black/white or blue/white.

Designs are all the same price.

Thank you for your letter.

Prices are: £6.00 per metre up to 50m
£5.50 per metre 50-100m
£5.00 over 100m

Over 200m, prices can be negotiated.

Terms: 30 days from date of delivery.

Design 18 which you asked for is no longer available.

Prices include carriage.

Figure 21. A list outline.

you can always leave something out later if you decide that it is not important or does not fit in.

Having made your list, you need to sort your points into a logical order. (For a discussion of what *is* a logical order, see below.) The best way to indicate the order is simply to number the points. An example of a list outline for a letter giving a customer a quotation is shown in figure 21.

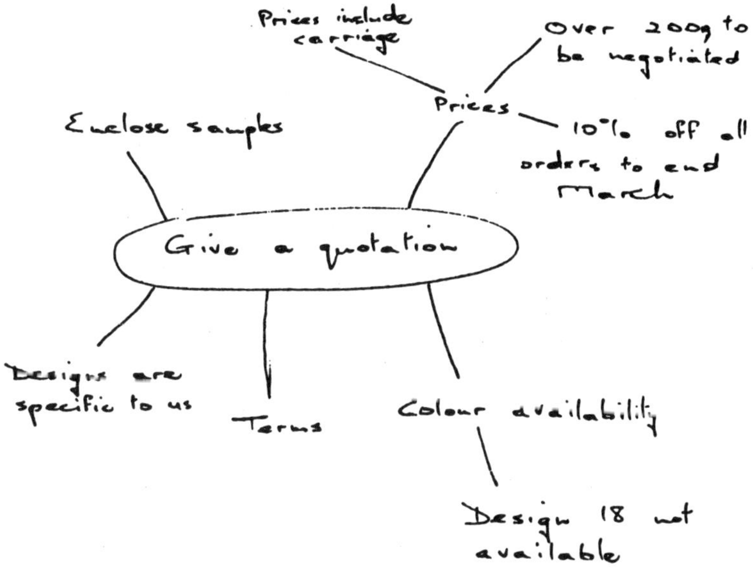


Figure 22. A chart outline.

A variation of this method, useful when doing a long report, involves using **index cards**. Instead of writing your ideas down in list form, write a heading on each card, with less important points under those headings. You can then shuffle them around into the order you want, without having to cope with a long, unwieldy list.

*Charting*

The second method of writing an outline is to draw a **chart**. This involves doing a rough diagram, with the main idea of the document in the centre and ideas for sections or paragraphs coming off it. It is rather like brainstorming—one idea leads to another. Once you have all the ideas down on your chart, you can either go straight on to writing your draft or number them in the order in which you want to present them, as with the second stage of listing. Figure 22 shows an example of a chart outline for the same letter as in figure 21.

*Freewriting*

Of the three methods of writing an outline, freewriting is probably the

I enclose samples of the different fabrics you asked for. You will be pleased to know that (there is a 10% discount on
* all orders which you place by the end of March).

* Each design is (special) to us, and will not be found on anyone else's fabrics. Designs are available as follows:

No. 41 in blue or green.
53 in grey/blue or brown/beige
62 in red only
67 in black/white or blue/white
* (18 is no longer available.)

Prices are as follows (all designs are the same price):

Up to 50 m – £6 per metre
* (Check) 50 – 100 m – £5.50 per metre
Over 100 m – £5 per metre
Over 200 m prices can be negotiated.

Prices include carriage, and our
* payment (        ) is 30 days from
* delivery (or is it invoice?)

Figure 23. A freewritten outline.

least used, but some people do prefer it to the others, so it is worth trying. It involves writing down everything that comes to you, without stopping but always bearing in mind your aim and your audience. Get everything down that you can think of, no matter how trivial, and do not worry about grammar or construction at this stage. If you know that your construction is wrong, leave it, but mark it to come back to. If you cannot think of the right word, leave a blank space, or use a less suitable word, but mark it. If you need to check any facts, mark them too, and go back.

Then go through what you have written, highlighting the important items and marking those points which are less important but should still be included. Delete anything which on second thoughts ought to be left out, and add any new information. Then either go straight into your draft, or number the points as in listing. An example of this method is shown in figure 23.

# J. PETERSON & CO

Paper Merchants

14 Union Road
Kingston Magna
Banshire
AB23 9VD
Tel. 897653

8 April 1995

Mr Roy Thompson
Clark & Co plc
Clark House
Devonshire Street
Manchester
M3 4KP

Dear Mr Thompson

I am extremely concerned about our order No. 456239 of 18 January for 20 Amstrad PC1512 double-drive computers. You may recall that we asked for delivery on 31 January.

I have chased you four times since then. I telephoned you when the delivery was a week overdue, on 7 February. On 4 March I telephoned you again, after you had promised to send replacements because five of the computers which were eventually delivered were single-drive machines. I telephoned yet again on 22 March when you failed to send an engineer to check two of the replacements, which were faulty. Finally I rang on 29 March when the two replacements you had promised failed to arrive.

In addition to the chasing I have had to do, I have had cause to complain twice. On 21 February I had to complain because the machines you delivered were not what we had ordered. I had to complain again on 13 March because of faults in the replacement machines.

Our first delivery arrived on 20 February, almost three weeks late, and it was wrong—you sent 15 double-drive and five single-drive machines. The second delivery came on 11 March, after I had chased you, and that was wrong as well, since two of the machines were faulty.

The result of all this is that we are still awaiting replacements for the two faulty machines, nearly three months after placing our initial order. I am coming under increasing pressure from my Directors to cancel the order, return the computers we have received and take our business elsewhere. I am reluctant to take such a step, so I would be grateful if you could look into the matter and telephone me within the next two days to tell me what you will be doing about it.

Yours sincerely

Emma Porter
Systems Manager

Figure 24. A letter outlining a sequence of events, with the points presented in ascending order of importance.

# J. PETERSON & CO

Paper Merchants

14 Union Road
Kingston Magna
Banshire
AB23 9VD
Tel. 897653

8 April 1994

Mr Roy Thompson
Clark & Co plc
Clark House
Devonshire Street
Manchester
M3 4KP

Dear Mr Thompson

I am extremely concerned about our order No. 456239 of 18 January for 20 Amstrad PC1512 double-drive computers. You may recall that we asked for delivery on 31 January.

On 7 February I had to chase you because the machines had not been delivered as requested.

On 20 February, nearly three weeks after our requested delivery date, we took delivery of 20 machines. Unfortunately, only 15 of them were double-drive. The other five were single-drive. I therefore telephoned you on 21 February and complained. You promised to send five double-drive machines and collect the single-drive ones.

On 4 March we had still not received the replacement machines, so I telephoned you and asked you to deliver them as soon as possible.

On 11 March the replacement machines were delivered, but two of them proved to be faulty. I therefore telephoned you on 13 March, and you promised to send an engineer to check them.

He had not arrived by 22 March, so I telephoned again. This time you said that you would send two replacement machines and collect the faulty ones.

On 29 March, when they had not arrived, I chased again, and was told by your secretary that they were on the way.

They have still not arrived, with the result that we have been waiting almost three months for our order to be fulfilled correctly.

I am coming under increasing pressure from my Directors to cancel the order, return the computers we have received and take our business elsewhere. I am reluctant to take such a step, so I would be grateful if you could look into the matter and telephone me within the next two days to tell me what you will be doing about it.

Yours sincerely

Emma Porter
Systems Manager

Figure 25. A letter outlining a sequence of events, with the points presented in chronological order.

## Achieving a logical progression

It was suggested above that you should sort out your points into a logical order. This is very important: unless you present your arguments or points in a logical sequence, unless your reader can follow easily from one point to the next, your document will lose its impact.

But what *is* a logical order? What is the best way to achieve a logical progression through your document? There are five ways in which you can assemble your points. With some documents you will find that only one is suitable. With others you may be able to choose one of two or three options. Choose the one which best suits the document you are writing, the audience it is aimed at and the result you want to achieve. Your options are:

- in chronological order;
- building up an argument by deduction, induction or both;
- in the same order as the document to which you are replying;
- in ascending order of importance;
- in descending order of importance.

The first method works well if you are describing a sequence of events, especially a complex one. In fact, if you are describing a sequence like that, it is it the only effective method to use. Look at the letters in figures 24 and 25. Which do you find easier to follow?

Figure 24 is written in ascending order of importance. After setting the scene by referring to her initial order, Emma Porter mentions the number of times she has chased Clark & Co, then the number of times she has complained. The next most important point is that the first delivery was late, then that the two deliveries were wrong in one way or another. Finally, she comes to the most important point—the fact that the mistakes have not been corrected.

However, although this might appear to be a logical sequence to follow, it is not effective for this particular letter, because it is difficult to see exactly where the fault lies, and how it arose.

Figure 25, on the other hand, brings up the points in chronological order. By spelling out the sequence, Emma makes it quite clear just how badly Clark & Co have treated her. You can follow the sequence of events, and you can see why certain actions were taken at certain times.

The second option is best used when you are arguing a case or trying to persuade someone to do something, as in a sales letter, or in

Date: 24 January 1995
To: All Directors
From: Ken Jameson
Subject: Appointment of an Administration Manager

We have now reduced the applicants for the above post to a shortlist of three. I have interviewed all three and they have gone through an assessment centre. Their CVs and assessment reports are attached for your information. All three are extremely well qualified for the post, but in very different ways. The following are my own assessments of the qualities of each candidate.

Judy Pearce has had a great deal of experience of managing people, as well as some administrative experience. From my interview and the assessment results, she appears to be a dominant personality, with firm ideas of how she would run the department. She tends to 'lead from the front'. She does not suffer fools gladly, but is very conscientious. I would expect her to ask a lot of her staff, but no more than she is prepared to do herself.

Hassan Ahmed has little experience of managing people, but he has a very sound knowledge of administrative practices, and is well informed about the latest developments in the field. He shows every sign of being able to develop the requisite 'people management' skills and would probably become a very committed manager, leading by example and by his knowledge of the subject.

Michael Hopwood has had a great deal of experience in managing a large department, and has the necessary skills in that area. He has no direct administrative knowledge, although he is currently on a course to acquire some. He appears to believe in a more 'democratic' style of management than the other two candidates, involving his whole department in the decisions that concern them. His assessment report indicates, however, that he is not afraid to assert his authority when the need arises.

All three candidates therefore have great strengths, but also, as one would expect, certain weaknesses.

We obviously need a manager who can motivate the department. We also need to take into account the present situation, both in the department and in the organisation as a whole. The staff in the department are of a very high calibre, and are prepared to commit themselves fully to the job. The organisation as a whole is committed to greater involvement of staff in the decision-making process. Administrative skills can be learned, but the right approach to staff management is something which to a large extent cannot be taught. I believe that Michael Hopwood has the right management approach as well as the ability to learn the administrative skills. I would therefore recommend that he be appointed to the post.

Figure 26. A memo showing the building of an argument by induction and deduction.

(2) I enclose samples of the different fabrics you asked for.

(13) There is 10% off all orders to the end of March.

(3) Each design is specific to us.

(4) Design 41 is available in blue or green.

(5) Design 53 is available in grey/blue or brown/beige.

(6) Design 62 is available in red only.

(7) Design 67 is available in black/white or blue/white.

(9) Designs are all the same price.

(1) Thank you for your letter.

(10) Prices are: £6.00 per metre up to 50m
£5.50 per metre 50–100m
£5.00 over 100m

(11) Over 200m, prices can be negotiated.

(14) Terms: 30 days from date of delivery

(8) Design 18 which you asked for is no longer available.

(12) Prices include carriage.

Figure 27. A listing outline numbered in ascending order of importance

some kinds of report. Figure 26 shows a memo giving a brief report, in which an argument is built up in this way. First Ken Jameson presents his assessments of the candidates, arrived at by induction. He then argues, by a process of deduction, for the candidate of his choice.

Presenting your points in the same order as the document to which you are replying obviously makes sense when you are answering a specific set of queries and not providing any extra information over and above what is asked for. If you are providing extra information, it can present problems as the extra information might not fit easily into this format. The problems are not insurmountable, however, and you

(2) I enclose samples of the different fabrics you asked for.

(3) There is 10 % off all orders to the end of March.

(14) Each design is specific to us.

(9) Design 41 is available in blue or green.

(10) Design 53 is available in grey/blue or brown/beige.

(11) Design 62 is available in red only.

(12) Design 67 is available in black/white or blue/white.

(4) Designs are all the same price.

(1) Thank you for your letter.

(5) Prices are: £6.00 per metre up to 50m
£5.50 per metre 50–100m
£5.00 over 100m

(6) Over 200m, prices can be negotiated.

(8) Terms: 30 days from date of delivery.

(13) Design 18 which you asked for is no longer available.

(7) Prices include carriage.

Figure 28. A listing outline numbered in descending order of importance.

may find that it is nevertheless the best format for your purposes.

Setting out your document in ascending or descending order of importance is relatively easy—provided, of course, that you are able to decide which are the most important points! The order you choose depends on the effect you want to achieve. If you decide on this kind of order, try numbering your points both in ascending and descending order, and see which looks better for your purposes.

Let us look again at the list outline shown in figure 21. Figure 27 shows the same list numbered in ascending order of importance, with the prices and terms—the most important points, since that was what

Dear Mr Carter

Thank you for your letter of 12 November enquiring about our fabrics and asking for a quotation. I enclose herewith samples of the different fabrics you asked for, which will give you an idea of the different designs. Each of the designs are unique to our range.

Colour availability is as follows: Design 41 is available in blue and green, Design 53 is available in grey and blue and brown and beige, Design 62 is available in red, and Design 67 is available in black and white and blue and white. Design 18 which you also asked about is no longer available. It has now gone out of fashion and been replaced by more up-to-date designs.

All the designs are the same price, and our price structure is as follows:

Up to 50 metres—£6.00 per metre
50-100 metres—£5.50 per metre
Over 100 metres—£5.00 per metre.

For any order over 200 metres, the price is subject to negotiation. Prices include carriage for delivery, and there is an additional 10 per cent off all orders, provided that they are received by ourselves before the end of January. Our payment terms are 30 days from date of delivery.

Yours sincerely

Martin Stacey
Sales Executive

Figure 29. A draft letter giving a quotation.

the customer requested—as the last items. Figure 28 shows it numbered in descending order, with these points at the beginning. Both are equally acceptable—it is a matter of personal taste and the effect you want to achieve. In the first, you will end up with a letter which builds up to the main point, whetting the customer's appetite as it were (or you could call it setting the scene) with the details of availability. In the second, your letter will answer the customer's immediate need—a quotation of prices and terms—with the details of availability and the uniqueness of the designs almost as an afterthought.

### Making your first draft

You are now ready to draft your letter. This involves organising your points into sentences and paragraphs that flow (see Chapter 4 for more on this), and tightening up your construction and points of grammar. Try to be as precise and to the point as possible, even though it is only a draft; you will find the editing easier later on.

If your document is long or complex, I would suggest that you type it, or have it typed. But whether you are writing it or having it typed, it should be double-spaced so that you can change it at the editing stage without making the whole thing illegible. Figure 29 shows the letter giving a quotation, which we outlined in figures 21-23, in draft form. There is still some polishing to do, as we will see in the next section, but you can see that it is taking shape in the right way.

### Editing your draft

Now your document must be 'polished'. Check your draft to see that it says everything that needs saying, but no more, and that it says it as concisely as possible. Editing is quite an art, and you can practise your skills on some of the letters, memos and reports that *you* receive: can you improve on them? There are a number of things to look for when editing your draft. The following questionnaire will help you identify any problems or errors.

*A checklist*

1. Is your document polite and unemotional?
2. Are there any unnecessary words or phrases? If you are not sure about particular phrases, try leaving them out. Does this affect the sense of what you are saying?
3. How would you react if *you* were receiving it? Is that the reaction you want from your audience?
4. Do you assume too much knowledge on the part of your reader?
5. Is it clear, or is anything ambiguous?
6. If it needs a reply, do you say so? Do you say by when?
7. Is it likely to achieve the result you want?
8. Have you included everything your reader needs to know?
9. Have you included points irrelevant to your aim or your audience?
10. Are the facts and arguments logically presented?
11. If you are presenting an argument, have you thought of all the counter-arguments?

# MASTERS & CO

*Fabric and Furnishings*

Masters House · Latherham · ST12 2BZ

Tel (01345) 98542 Fax (01345) 54371

19 November 1994

Mr L. Carter
Bennett and Turner Ltd
43 Union Street
Stampton
BR8 7JJ

Dear Mr Carter

Thank you for your enquiry of 12 November. I enclose samples of the different fabrics you asked for. Each of the designs shown is unique to our range.

The designs are available in the following colours: Design 41 in blue or green; Design 53 in grey and blue or brown and beige; Design 42 in red only; and Design 67 in black and white or blue and white. I am afraid that Design 18 is no longer available.

All the designs are the same price, and our prices are as follows:
Up to 50 metres – £6.00 per metre
50-100 metres – £5.50 per metre
Over 100 metres – £5.00 per metre.
For orders over 200 metres, the price is subject to negotiation. All these prices include carriage. Our payment terms are 30 days from date of delivery.

We are giving an additional 10 per cent discount on all orders received before the end of January, so if you would like to place an order, why not do so soon and take advantage of this offer?

If you would like any further information please don't hesitate to contact me.

Yours sincerely

Martin Stacey
Sales Executive

Figure 30. A letter based on the draft in figure 29.

Make any changes you think necessary on the draft itself, so that you end up with an amended draft. From this you can write the final document. Figure 30 shows the final quotation letter that Martin Stacey might have written. Can you spot the changes?

- He has corrected a few grammatical errors (like 'Each of the designs *is* unique' instead of '*are*') and changed a few punctuation marks to make the list in the second paragraph easier to follow.

- He has edited out unnecessary words and phrases like 'which will give you an idea of the different designs' in the first paragraph, and 'for delivery' at the end (carriage means delivery).

- He has changed the wording in the first sentence and in the sentence about the extra discount, to reduce the number of words in each.

- He has changed the wording and layout of the second paragraph so as to avoid any ambiguity (the way it was expressed in the draft, it was not clear whether, for example, Design 41 was available both in blue and in grey, or in a combination of blue and grey).

- He has cut out the explanation for the non-availability of Design 18. It is not really necessary for the customer to know why it has been withdrawn. The explanation as it stands could be interpreted as insulting—suggesting that the customer is out of touch with fashion.

- He has put the sentence about the extra discount at the beginning of a new paragraph to give it more emphasis. He has also made the ending rather more friendly and encouraging. The combination of these two changes should give the letter more chance of achieving its objective—to get the customer to place an order.

## CHECKLIST

- What is your aim in writing your document?

- Do you know precisely what you want to achieve, and how you want your audience to react?
- What are your readers like—what is their level of intelligence, how deep is their knowledge, what is important to them?
- Are you being polite and unemotional?
- Do you have all the information you need? Is it correct?
- Have you assembled all your arguments? What about the counter-arguments?
- Which is the best way of presenting your points, both for your document and for your audience?
- Which method of writing an outline suits you best?
- Do you know how to edit your draft into a clear, concise document that achieves your objective?

# 3
# Laying Out Documents

The way that you lay out your document can help or hinder your reader's understanding. A poorly laid out communication will usually be difficult to follow, but by giving a little thought to its appearance, even if the basic words and structures are the same, you can actually make it easier to read.

Poor layout can also reflect badly on you. Although business communication is generally becoming more informal, there are still certain right ways of doing things; if you do not follow them your work will look slipshod and unprofessional to others.

## LAYING OUT LETTERS

Letters are perhaps the most important communications to get right because they officially represent your company or organisation to the outside world. Sloppy work reflects badly not only on you, but on the organisation you represent.

### Designing letterheads

Your letterhead is the part of your letter with which you have more scope than with any other. There is no set way of displaying letterheads, as you will notice simply by looking at the array of styles that cross your desk in a week. It is worth taking some trouble over the design of your letterhead, as it can in many ways dictate the sort of image you present. You might also consider adopting a **house style**, with the same **logo** or style of lettering appearing on all your stationery, on your vans, on your premises, on your advertisements—in fact everywhere that your company name appears.

Whatever style you choose, your letterheads should be very clear. They should give your correspondents all the information they might need if they want to contact you: your company name, your address, your telephone and fax numbers. In addition, there are certain legal obligations which apply to limited companies.

**Formatting your letter**

The format of your letter is important. It should follow certain conventions and a certain order.

*1. The date*

This used to be shown as 23rd October, 1994, but is now almost always shown as 23 October 1994, without the 'th' after the day, and without a comma after the month.

*2. Your reference*

It is not essential to include a reference, but it can help you retrieve a letter from your filing system. If you do have one, it will usually be the initials of the person who dictated the letter and those of the person who typed it, as in TRM/HGS. It can also include a file or account number, for example TRM/HGS/83/4.

*3. Your correspondent's reference*

Use it if they have quoted one.

*4. The 'inside address'*

The name and address of the person to whom the letter is being sent. This is important, because if you do not put it in, it will be difficult later to remember to whom the letter went.

*5. The letter itself*

The various elements of the letter are discussed in the sections that follow.

*6. Any notes about enclosures or copies*

If you are enclosing something with your letter, you should type 'Enc.' at the bottom. If you are sending a copy to another person you should type 'cc' and the person's name at the bottom. The following abbreviations may be typed on copies of the letter, but not on the original: bcc (**blind carbon copy**) if you are sending a copy to someone else without the original addressee knowing; and fyi (for your information) if you are sending a copy to someone purely for information.

**CORFIELD DISTRICT COUNCIL**

Council Offices
Diston Road
Corfield
Somerset
TA45 6BN
Tel. (01732) 68832

23 November 1994

Mr James Baker,
Managing Director,
Corfield Cleaning Services,
68 King Street,
Corfield,
TA45 2VC.

Dear Mr Baker,

When you won the contract for the cleaning of all council premises, we drew up a very specific schedule of what was required in each building.

I regret to say that, in the few weeks that the contract has been in operation, your company does not appear to have been sticking to that schedule as precisely as we would wish. I enclose a list of shortcomings which our wardens and caretakers have noticed over the last two weeks. As you will see, the problems are not confined to one particular building, which seems to indicate that there is some misunderstanding over the interpretation of the contract, rather than that one or two employees are not doing the job thoroughly.

I am sure you will understand our concern that the service you are offering is below the standard expected so soon after the start of your contract. I would be grateful therefore if you would look into the problem and let me know as soon as possible what corrective action you propose to take.

Yours sincerely

Patricia May
Director of Services

Figure 31. A letter set out in fully displayed format, with full punctuation.

There are three main ways of setting out your letter, and two styles of punctuation. The ways of setting it out are:

- the fully displayed or indented style;
- the blocked style;
- the semi-blocked style

The two styles of punctuation are:

- full punctuation;
- open punctuation.

## Letter layouts

In the **fully displayed** style, the first line of each paragraph is indented. The date usually appears on the right-hand side of the page. An example of this style is shown in figure 31. This is the traditional way of setting out a letter but it is now used less and less because, with all the indenting and setting out required, it takes longer to type.

The **blocked** style is the most common format nowadays. In this format everything, from the date to the signature, is ranged on the left-hand margin. There is no indenting; new paragraphs are identified by leaving a line space. Figure 32 is an example of this style. It is popular because it is quicker. No time-consuming layout is required—everything starts at one margin.

The **semi-blocked** format is very similar to the blocked. However, the date is shown on the right-hand side, to make it easier to see when looking for the letter in a filing system. Some semi-blocked letters also place the complimentary close ('Yours sincerely' or 'Yours faithfully') in the centre of the page, to make the letter look more attractive.

## Punctuation

**Full punctuation**, as its name implies, means that all punctuation marks are shown. There is a comma at the end of each line of the inside address except the last, which has a full stop; there are commas after the salutation ('Dear Mr Brown') and after 'Yours sincerely' or 'Yours faithfully'; and there are full stops between the letters of abbreviations like VAT or MBE. Figure 31, as well as being fully displayed, has full punctuation.

**Open punctuation** means that punctuation marks are kept to a minimum. Although they are used in the body of the letter through

**JOHNSON BRYANT & CO**
ESTATE AGENTS
4 High Street
Lackington
LA2 5TG
Tel. (01392) 43582

6 April 1995

Mr Keith Sargent
7 Laburnum Grove
Lackington
LA4 6GH

Dear Mr Sargent

Following our meeting yesterday, we would be delighted to act for you in the sale of your house, at an asking price of £120,000. Our commission is 1 per cent of the sale price, payable on completion of the sale. Someone will call in the next day or two to erect a 'For Sale' sign.

May I take this opportunity to thank you for placing your house in our hands, and to assure you that we will do everything we can to achieve a quick sale.

Yours sincerely

Peter Johnson

Figure 32. A letter set out in blocked format, with open punctuation

grammatical necessity, there are no punctuation marks in the inside address, no commas after the salutation or the complimentary close and no full stops between the letters of abbreviation. Figure 32, as well as being blocked, also has open punctuation.

### Styles of address

It is important to get the name and job title of your correspondent right. If you are replying to a letter, address the person in the form in which he or she has signed. So if someone has signed his letter John Smith, you should address him as John Smith, not J. Smith.

But what do you do if you are replying to a handwritten letter and you cannot decipher the handwriting? The best thing you can do is make a guess at the name and address and start your letter:

'I hope I have the name and address right. Please excuse me if I have misread your writing.'

Do *not* say:

'I could not read your writing.'

That will put your reader in the wrong, and put your communication on a bad footing.

There are three ways of addressing a man, and two ways of addressing a woman. Men can be addressed as:

James Robinson Esq.
Mr James Robinson
James Robinson

Women can be addressed as:

Miss (or Mrs or Ms) Susan Brown
Susan Brown

Which should you use, and under what circumstances?

The use of Esq (short for Esquire) is now very much rarer than it was. It is a very formal form of address, and although it is still used, it is generally considered a little old fashioned. It is, however, still considered polite to use some form of title (Mr, Mrs, Miss, Rev, Dr), although it is becoming more and more common to address people simply as Susan Brown, James Robinson etc. As a rule, you should always address a member of the general public as Mr, Mrs etc, but when writing to business contacts you have a choice. A title is slightly more formal, and should therefore be used when addressing people you have not previously met. If you have met them, you should be able to judge for yourself whether they will be offended it you leave the title out, or whether they are likely to regard you as a bit stuffy if you use it.

Addressing a woman can sometimes be tricky. It used to be common for women to indicate their marital status with their signature, as in:

Yours sincerely
Margaret James (Mrs)

But many women nowadays, particularly in business, simply sign their names, without indicating their marital status. In these circumstances, you should address them as Ms (Ms Susan Brown). This is becoming increasingly common and acceptable as a form of address. Some women are still slightly offended by this relatively new term, however, so if your correspondent signs herself Mrs or Miss, then use the same form of address in your reply.

What do you do if you do not even know what sex your correspondent is? If someone signs simply J. Robinson, you have a problem. The best thing to do is to try to guess whether the person is a man or a woman and address your letter accordingly. You should then start your letter

'I hope it *is* Mr (or Ms) Robinson. Your letter was just signed J. Robinson, so I am not sure.'

How should you address your letter if you are writing to a company or organisation, rather than to a named individual? Wherever possible, address it to a particular person in the organisation, by job title if you do not know his or her name. So, for example, if you had a sales query, you would address your letter to the Sales Manager. If it were a complaint about an unpaid account, you would write to the Accountant. A letter to your local council about a planning application would be addressed to the Chief Planning Officer. If you do not know who in the organisation might deal with your letter, here are some guidelines to help you.

1. If you are writing to a company, address your letter to the Manager or the Managing Director.
2. If you are writing to a club or a professional institution, address it to the Secretary.
3. If you are writing to a firm with a sole owner, address it to the Proprietor.
4. If you are writing to a local authority, address it to the Chief Executive.
5. If you are writing to a government department, address it to the Minister or to the Permanent Secretary.
6. Only if writing to a partnership do you not address your letter to a particular person. The correct way to address a partnership is Messrs, as in Messrs Black and Green.

### The salutation

The salutation is the part which opens a letter (which 'salutes' your correspondent): the part which begins 'Dear...'. If you know your correspondent, there should be no problem deciding on the best salutation. If you know him or her well, you could begin 'Dear John' or 'Dear Mary'. If you do not want to be quite so informal, you should use their title: 'Dear Mr Black' or 'Dear Miss White'. One thing you should *not* do is address someone whose name you know as 'Dear Sir' or 'Dear Madam'. This is so formal and unfriendly as to be almost rude.

A sort of 'halfway house' between these two degrees of formality is becoming increasingly common. It involves using no title in the inside address, and using the person's full name in the salutation. For example the inside address would be 'Mary White' rather than 'Miss Mary White' and the salutation would be 'Dear Mary White'. The implication is that, although you are not on first name terms yet, you expect to be fairly soon—perhaps because you are about to develop a business relationship. But if you use it, do so sparingly. It is not yet fully accepted, and some people might be offended by it. This style of salutation is also used sometimes when a woman has not indicated her marital status, instead of using Ms.

If you do not know your correspondent's name, the correct salutation is 'Dear Sir or Madam' (or 'Dear Sir/Madam'). So in all cases where you are addressing someone by their job title only, you should use this form of salutation. It used to be common to write just 'Dear Sir', but this is no longer acceptable, as many business people and top administrators are women; they will quite rightly feel offended by being address as 'Sir'. Some people try to get around the formality and clumsiness of 'Dear Sir or Madam' but writing 'Dear Managing Director' or 'Dear Sales Manager', but this is not a common usage, and sounds as clumsy as 'Dear Sir or Madam'.

If you are writing to a partnership, and have therefore addressed them as 'Messrs Black and Green', the correct form of salutation is 'Dear Sirs'. There is as yet no generally accepted non-sexist alternative to this—'Dear Sirs or Madams' does not sound right! And, of course, Messrs, being the plural of Mr, is itself sexist. You could get round the problem by addressing your letter to

The Senior Partner
Black and Green

and starting it 'Dear Sir or Madam'. This is not strictly correct, but it is unlikely to cause offence.

## Beginning your letter

The way you begin your letter is important. Set the tone for the rest of the letter early, and signpost what it is going to be about. You can use a heading if you think it will help clarify the subject immediately; however a heading does tend to make a letter rather formal, and headings are used less now than they used to be.

If you are replying to a letter from your correspondent, then a simple way of indicating the subject is to say

Thank you for your letter of 20 March about the trade exhibition.

In order to get a good reaction from your readers, you need to make them *want* to read your letters. You must therefore get their attention and interest early on in the letter, and this is why your opening is so important. For this reason do avoid tired old clichés like

With reference to your letter of 20 March...
I am writing to tell you...

Even 'Thank you for your letter of 20 March' can be avoided with a little thought. Here are a few possible alternatives:

I was delighted to receive your letter of 20 March about...

I was very sorry to hear from your letter of 20 March that...

Thank you for taking the trouble to write and tell me about...

I was concerned to read your letter of 20 March, and to hear that you have been having problems with...

I have thought carefully about the points you raised in your letter of 20 March and...

There are of course many ways of starting your letters—almost as many ways as there are subjects to write about. But do make the start of your letter relevant to your subject *and* interesting, rather than using some of the forms that have been used over and over again.

Of course, if you are not replying to a letter, you can get into your subject straight away, which makes it easier to avoid clichés. But set the tone as well as the subject from the start. Your reader should be able to tell from the opening not only what the letter is about, but also what your attitude is.

### The body of your letter

The main body of your letter should follow logically on from your opening, and there should be a logical flow through the letter to the end. The techniques for achieving this were discussed in Chapter 2.

The construction and style of your letter will be discussed in Chapters 4, 5 and 6. For the moment, let us just say that, apart from flowing logically, it should follow the three rules of business communication and be brief, clear and direct.

**Ending your letter**

Your closing paragraph is as important as your opening. This is the last thing your correspondent will read, and the last impression he or she will be left with. You should use it for two purposes:

- to **summarise** your position;
- to indicate any **action** that needs to be taken, and by whom.

Summarising your position does not mean you should provide a summary of everything you have said; that would be boring. You should simply summarise your views, or how you want your reader to feel. The exact wording you use will obviously depend on the type of letter, but here are a few examples of different summary endings:

I hope this has helped you to understand our position.
These are the problems I would like to review when we meet.
I think you will agree that this is a very special offer.
I am sure you will appreciate our concern over this matter.

There are five different kinds of action ending, depending on the kind of response you expect.

*Positive reader response*

This means that you expect the reader to take some action. Typical endings of this kind include:

I would be grateful if you could let me know as soon as possible what action you intend to take.

I look forward to hearing from you.

Perhaps you could give me your views on these proposals within the next week or so.

Please let me have your cheque in settlement of this account.

*Positive writer response.*

This means that *you* you will be taking some action. For example:

I will thoroughly investigate the problem and contact you as soon as I have an answer.

I will consider your proposals carefully, and let you have my response within the next few days.

I am waiting to hear from my accountant, and will be in touch as soon as I do.

*Passive reader response*
This means that the reader has the option of taking some action if he or she wants to, but that you do not expect it. Typical endings might be:

If you need any further information, do let me know.

If I can be of any further assistance, please get in touch.

If I do not hear from you within the next two weeks, I will assume that you are happy with the new arrangements.

*Passive writer response*
This means that you *might* take some action. Typical endings might be:

I will contact you if the situation changes.

If I receive any further information, I will let you know.

*No response*
If you do not want to continue the correspondence under any circumstances, then you should make this clear—not in so many words, as that would be impolite, but by your closing line. Here are a few examples:

Thank you for writing.

I am grateful for your views.

I found your comments interesting, and will bear them in mind for the future.

All of these indicate quite clearly that your reader should not expect to hear from you again, and that you do not expect to hear any more from them. But they all do so in a courteous and friendly way.

*Adding a courtesy line*
Finally, you can add a courtesy line if you wish or if it is appropriate. It is not always necessary, but you might feel that it suits your aim and your subject to include one. Typical examples are:

Thank you for your co-operation.
I apologise for the inconvenience you have been caused.
I look forward to a long and profitable business relationship.

But avoid what are called **participial phrases**, which are so often used to end letters. Do not say

Hoping to hear from you soon.

*or*

Thanking you for your help in this matter.

It is bad grammar and looks sloppy. There is no reason why you cannot use a full sentence:

I hope to hear from you soon.

*or*

Thank you for your help.

You can, of course, combine a summary, an action ending and perhaps a courtesy line in one sentence. You could, for example say:

> These are the problems as I see them, and I would be grateful if you could let me know as soon as possible how you intend to deal with them.
>
> I am sure you will understand our concern over the delay in paying, and I look forward to receiving your cheque within the next few days.
>
> I apologise for the inconvenience you have been caused, but I hope that the arrangements I have made will go some way towards alleviating the problem.

### The complimentary close

The complimentary close is the 'signing off' part of the letter—the part that usually says 'Yours faithfully' or 'Yours sincerely'. In fact these two forms are the only ones you really need to know—but you do need to know which to use under which circumstances.

The rule is quite simple. If your salutation is 'Dear Sir or Madam', then your complimentary close should be 'Yours faithfully'. If your salutation is 'Dear Mr Brown', 'Dear Mrs Green' or 'Dear Robin', then your complimentary close should be 'Yours sincerely'. 'Yours truly' was once quite common, but it now looks very old fashioned. Even more old fashioned is

| | |
|---|---|
| I am<br>Yours faithfully | I remain<br>Yours sincerely |

If you are being very informal, and writing to someone you know well, you can use 'With kind regards', 'With best wishes' or some such informal wording.

There should then be a space for the signature, and then the name of the signatory. If you are writing to someone you know well, who already knows your position in the company, then it is not necessary to put your job title. But if you are writing to a member of the public, or to someone with whom you have not had dealings before, you should put your position under your name, as in

Catherine Smythe
Managing Director

Some people put the name of the company above the name of the signatory, as in:

for ROBERTS AND DAVIDSON LTD
Ken Stephens
Sales Director

This is supposed to indicate that the person signing is authorised to sign on behalf of the company, but it is becoming less and less common, and has an old-fashioned look.

Sometimes a letter may be dictated by one person, but signed by another, usually a secretary. For example the Marketing Director might dictate a number of letters before going off on a sales trip, and leave them to be typed and signed by her secretary. In that case the secretary would type the Marketing Director's name and title as usual, but would sign them herself and put a small pp for *per procurationem* (by proxy) before her signature, thus:

Yours sincerely

*pp Jane Harrison*

Sarah Morgan
Marketing Director

### When to add special clauses

Depending on the sort of letter you are writing, there may be standard clauses which you need to include to safeguard your legal position.

These could include exclusion clauses in contractual letters, or maintenance clauses when you are hiring equipment. Make sure that you know whether any such standard clauses apply to your business, and if in any doubt, take legal advice.

## LAYING OUT MEMOS

Some companies have preprinted memo forms, while others have a house style for the layout of memos. There are several different formats, but they all have the same elements:

- the name of the writer;
- the name of the addressee;
- the date;
- the subject;
- the body of the memo.

The first three should of course go at the top, but the order you put them in is up to you. So you might write in any of these forms:

To: David Cousins<br>
From: Simon Kitchener<br>
Date: 22 May 1995

From: Simon Kitchener Date: 22 May 1995<br>
To: David Cousins

Date: 22 May 1995<br>
To: David Cousins<br>
From: Simon Kitchener

You don't have to use a heading in a memo, but it is sometimes a good idea to do so; it tells your reader what the memo is going to be about, and it saves you having to explain the subject in the memo itself. Your memo might, for example, read

To: David Cousins<br>
From: Simon Kitchener<br>
Date: 22 May 1995

ARRANGEMENTS FOR GRADUATE INTERVIEWS

This tells your reader immediately what to expect. It also saves you

To: Janet Mitchell
From: Suresh Govinder
Date: 24 March 1995

IMPROVEMENTS IN DISTRIBUTION

You asked me last week to look at ways in which we might be able to improve the quality of our service to customers.

I have examined our internal systems, and found that there is a high degree of inflexibility within our warehouse. Packers, for example, do not pick items from the shelves, and pickers do not pack parcels. So a packer might be struggling to keep up with the workload while the picker is 'coasting' , or vice versa. This means of course that the customer's parcel takes as long as the slowest link in the chain.

I have also looked at the service our carriers provide, and compared it with the competition. Our present carriers, XYZ, aim to provide a two-day service, but they do not guarantee it, and from the complaints we have received from customers, it looks as though they quite often do not achieve it. Most of the carriers who do guarantee a two-day service are slightly more expensive. The cheapest is Speeditruk. On our present throughput, I estimate that changing to them would cost us an extra £1,000 per year.

In view of the fact that we are obviously losing customers because of the slowness of our distribution, I think that we ought to be changing both our internal systems and our carriers. There is no apparent reason why we cannot reorganise the warehouse staff into flexible teams, where each person does whatever needs doing at a particular time. This would mean that if there were an overload in the picking area, packers could be diverted to help relieve it, and vice versa. Such a reorganisation would cost us nothing, but would make us very much more efficient, and could save as much as a day in turning orders around.

Although changing carriers would increase our costs, the increase would not be very significant, and if it stops the flow of customers to other suppliers, it would be worthwhile. I therefore suggest that we terminate our contract with XYZ and negotiate a new one with Speeditruk.

Figure 33. How a memo should be laid out.

having to include a sentence such as 'I would like to discuss this year's arrangements for graduate interviews.'

The body of the memo consists of your arguments, or the points you want to make. Your heading might provide all the introduction you need, but you might have to write a short introductory paragraph as well, giving some of the background to your memo. Your last paragraph should indicate what action you want taken, your conclusions or recommendations or a summary of your arguments. Figure 33 shows all these elements in a fairly simple memo.

## LAYING OUT REPORTS

Reports can serve a wide variety of purposes, and so have a number of different formats. Most reports, however, follow the same basic pattern, regardless of the subject or aim. This pattern is:

- the preliminary pages;
- the introduction;
- the body of the report;
- the conclusion, recommendations or main findings;
- acknowledgements;
- appendices.

### Types of report

There are three main categories of report, each with a slight variation on the basic pattern.

*Recommendation reports*

As their name suggests, these are written with the aim of recommending some kind of action. They may include a conclusion or conclusions as well as recommendations, but need not always do so.

*Conclusion reports*

A feasibility study is an example of a conclusion report. You might be asked to look into the feasibility of a certain course of action; you would reach a conclusion as to whether it was a viable proposition or not. You would not, however, make any recommendations.

*Information reports*

These are reports which only present information. You might be briefing someone or providing background information, and you would probably present your main findings (or highlights), but

MANAGEMENT STRUCTURES

AT

GUNTON ENGINEERING LTD

by

Yvonne Macdonald

24 November 1994

To: All Directors and Managers

Figure 34. An example of the title page of a report.

because of the nature of the report, it would contain no conclusion or recommendations.

## Preliminary pages of a report

Before your report itself starts, you need to provide certain information, and this should be done in the preliminary pages. These pages should be:

*1. The title page*

This should give the title of the report, who it is by, the date it was written and the distribution. A typical title page might look like the one shown in figure 34.

SUMMARY

The current management structure at Gunton's is hierarchical, with a great deal of direction from above.

There is strong evidence that this causes resentment in the junior ranks. There is also evidence to suggest that the structure leads to 'empire building'. Both these factors appear to have a deadening effect on initiative and creativity.

A more flexible structure would alleviate these problems but it would require a complete revision of responsibilities, and would cause disruption in the short term. It would, moreover, require a complete change in management style and attitude, from the top down.

However, if the changes were well planned and handled sympathetically, the disruption could be kept to a minimum, and they would undoubtedly result in greater efficiency and improved morale.

If the company is to meet the challenges of the future and remain competitive, I believe it is essential that the changes are made.

Figure 35. An example of a report summary.

*2. A summary*
If the report is a long one, it is a good idea to provide a brief summary (no more than 150 words), giving the gist of what the report contains, and the main conclusions, recommendations or findings. This helps busy executives, who may not want (or need) to work through the whole report to see at a glance what it is about. This should be on a page by itself, headed 'Summary'. An example of a summary is shown in figure 35.

*3. A table of contents*
This is also only necessary if the report is a long one, and should also be on a page by itself. In it you should list the major headings and the pages on which they appear.

## Writing an introduction to a report
In your introduction, give the background to the report itself—why it was written, what it is about, who it is intended for, who asked for it, and the investigative and other methods used.

INTRODUCTION

I was asked by the Managing Director to investigate the management structures at Gunton's Engineering Ltd, to find out whether they are still appropriate in view of recent developments within the company and in the business environment, and to make recommendations for any changes I thought were necessary.

This report, which is intended as a discussion document for all Directors and Managers, is the result of my investigations. I was asked particularly to address it to Managers as well as Directors, as it was felt that my conclusions should be seen and discussed by everyone who might be affected by them.

I looked carefully at the present structure, how it was established and how it has evolved. Over a period of four weeks, I watched management in action by attending meetings, including Board meetings, and by sitting in on formal and informal one-to-one and group discussions between Managers and Directors.

I then discussed with every Manager and Director their views on the structure, and what they saw as its strengths and weaknesses. I also canvassed their views on alternative models, and how they might apply to Gunton's. I obtained the opinions of non-management staff through the Staff Council and Trade Union representatives.

My conclusions and recommendations are based on my assessment of the present structure and how it affects all aspects of the company's performance, together with my assessment of the attitudes of the Managers, Directors and other staff and of the alternative models which might be applied.

Figure 36. An example of an introduction to a report.

Be careful that you *only* give the background to the report. There can be a temptation to let the introduction merge into the body of the report. Use the following checklist to ensure that your introduction contains all the information it should, but nothing else.

1. Is it all in the past tense? If not, it is likely that some of it belongs in the body of the report.

2. Is it clear why the report was written?

3. Do you say who it was written for?

4. Does it give an idea of the subject of the report *without* giving details of the actual investigation or the conclusions or recommendations?

Look at figure 36, which shows an example of an introduction. Bear in mind that the nature of the introduction will depend very much on the subject and nature of the report itself.

### Writing the body of the report

The body of the report is the largest part, and this is where you set out all the relevant information what you have discovered during your investigation, the facts on which you base your argument, the details that you have been asked to provide.

Your report should follow a logical pattern, as outlined under **Achieving a logical progression** in Chapter 2. The particular pattern you adopt will depend on the nature of the report. An analytical report should usually develop a logical argument, building up to a conclusion and/or recommendations. A briefing report would probably have the sections set out in order of priority. But there might be reports which are better laid out in chronological sequence. Reports can also be sectionalised, each section dealing with a different department or field of activity, but each section will still need to follow one of the above patterns. So before you start writing your report, make sure that you choose the most appropriate format for your purposes.

'Don't worry, I'll boil it down to a one-page summary.'

*Tips on setting out a report*
How you actually set out your report depends on how long it is, and what it is to be used for. Here are a few tips.

- If it is a long report, you should use **headed sections**. Start each new section on a new page, like the chapters of a book. This looks better, and is easier to absorb, than a long mass of text.
- If it is not long enough to sectionalise in this way, you should still consider using headings within the text.
- If it is fairly complex, you might use different **weights of heading**, rather like the headings in this book—say block capitals for main headings, underlining for subheadings.
- If people are likely to want to refer to specific paragraphs (or if you need to cross-refer from one paragraph to another), then you might **number the paragraphs**.
- Another way of differentiating paragraphs in a complex document is to use different **numbering systems**. Your headings could be numbered 1,2,3 etc, sub-paragraphs under those headings 1.1, 1.2, 1.3, 2.1, 2.2 etc, and sub-sub-paragraphs 1.1.1, 1.1.2 etc. Another way to is to number sub-paragraphs (a), (b), (c) etc, and sub-sub-paragraphs (i), (ii), (iii) etc. Figures 37 and 38 show a section of a report numbered in these ways.

## The conclusion, recommendations or main findings

Some people prefer to put their conclusions and recommendations at the *beginning* of their report, immediately after the introduction. Their readers can then see what they have concluded and then the background information on which the recommendation or conclusion is based. I do not recommend this order, however, particularly if you think some of your readers might resist your conclusions. If they see and disagree with your conclusion before reading the facts on which it is based, they may well look at the facts with a jaundiced eye, trying to pick holes in your arguments. It is better (and more logical) for them to look at the facts first. That, after all, is how you yourself will have reached your conclusion, so that is the way to lead your readers to the same conclusion.

If this section consists of your main findings or highlights from the report rather than a conclusion—in other words if it is something like a briefing report, which does not present an argument—then there is perhaps not the same need to put it at the end. However, I would still

3. THE CONDUCT OF MEETINGS

The way in which meetings are conducted at Gunton's varies considerably, depending on their composition. I have classified the meetings into three groups, each of which has a different composition, and each of which is therefore conducted in a different way.

3.1. *Peer Group Meetings*
These are meetings between people at roughly the same level in the organisation: directors with directors, senior managers with senior managers, junior managers with junior managers, supervisors with supervisors.

3.1.1. Discussion at these meetings is usually vigorous, with a high level of participation. Participants are not generally apprehensive about putting their views (but see Paragraph 3.1.2 below), and conclusions are reached only after all sides of the argument have been heard.

3.1.2. It is noticeable, however, that the lower down the scale of seniority the participants are, the more restricted their deliberations are. Discussion is still vigorous, but it does not necessarily cover all aspects of the subject. A meeting of junior managers, for example, discussed at length how they might improve communications at their level. At a certain point, it became obvious that policy aspects were involved; at that point the discussion veered away, as if the participants were by mutual agreement avoiding giving their opinions on matters which were outside their own narrow areas of responsibility. The result was that what might have been useful changes in the patterns of communication at lower management level were not considered.

Figure 37. One way of numbering paragraphs in a report.

prefer to see it there. If your main findings appear at the beginning, your readers will be tempted to read only them, and to skip the rest. But if your report has been written properly, there should be nothing in it which is not necessary, so those readers who skip the body of the report will miss some important information. Moreover, a section of main findings or highlights at the end serves as a useful summation and reminder of what has gone before.

In an investigative or analytical report, you may discover several possible solutions to the problem you have been investigating. You may, of course, only *recommend* one solution, but you should give all the possibilities in your conclusion, with their advantages and disadvantages.

3. THE CONDUCT OF MEETINGS

The way in which meetings are conducted at Gunton's varies considerably, depending on their composition. I have classified the meetings into three groups, each of which has a different composition, and each of which is therefore conducted in a different way.

(a) *Peer Group Meetings*. These are meetings between people at roughly the same level in the organisation: directors with directors, senior managers with senior managers, junior managers with junior managers, supervisors with supervisors.

(i) Discussion at these meetings is usually vigorous, with a high level of participation. Participants are not generally apprehensive about putting their views (but see Paragraph (ii) below), and conclusions are reached only after all sides of the argument have been heard.

(ii) It is noticeable, however, that the lower down the scale of seniority the participants are, the more restricted their deliberations are. Discussion is still vigorous, but it does not necessarily cover all aspects of the subject. A meeting of junior managers, for example, discussed at length how they might improve communications at their level. At a certain point, it became obvious that policy aspects were involved; at that point the discussion veered away, as if the participants were by mutual agreement avoiding giving their opinions on matters which were outside their own narrow areas of responsibility. The result was that what might have been useful changes in the patterns of communication at lower management level were not considered.

Figure 38. An alternative way of numbering paragraphs in a report.

If your report is to contain both a conclusion and recommendations, then put them in two separate sections. It only makes the report confusing if you try to combine both a conclusion and recommendations in one section.

Your recommendations should follow logically from the facts and arguments you have presented earlier in the report. Always give your reasons for recommending a particular course of action, especially if you have proposed several possible solutions in your conclusion and are recommending just one. If you are making more than one recommendation they should be numbered, to make them clearer and easier to differentiate.

Do be very specific in your recommendations. It is no good saying, 'I recommend that the management structure of Gunton's be changed', or even 'I recommend that the management structure of Gunton's be made more flexible, with greater responsibility for junior managers.' What exactly does this mean? Say more specifically *what* the new structure should be and *how* it should be brought in. Or, at the very least, recommend that the structure be changed and that a working party be set up (specifying its composition and terms of reference) to see how best to introduce it. Could you also suggest a timescale for introducing the measures recommended? Your report is less likely to be politely ignored or shelved if you make your recommendations specific and give them a timescale.

**Including acknowledgements**

Do you plan to use material from any other source in your report? If so you should acknowledge it. Do not try to pass someone else's work off as your own. Not only is it dishonest, but if you are found out, it will discredit everything you have written, even the parts that *are* your own work.

But you do not want to clutter up the body of the report with acknowledgements—they will interrupt the flow of your argument. So if you do need to acknowledge the help of other people, or if you have referred to their written work, you need a separate acknowledgements section.

How you lay it out is to a large extent a matter of personal preference. Do you just want to thank certain people for their help in compiling the report? If so you can simply say:

> I would like to acknowledge the help of the following people in the compilation of this report:

and then list their names. Alternatively, you can actually mention what help they gave you.

If you have referred to documents and publications, then it is customary to give the following information:

- In the case of books, the author, the title, the publisher, and usually the year of publication (shown in the copyright information of the book), eg Smith, P.J. *Business Organisation*, Jones & Co, London, 1990.
- In the case of magazine or journal articles, the author, the title of the article, the title of the magazine or journal, the volume and number (or date) of the particular issue, and usually the

year of publication, e.g Smith, P.J. 'Organising an Accounting System', *Small Trader*, Vol 7, No 12, 1992.

- In the case of government documents, the department or author, the title, the document number if there is one, the publisher (usually HMSO) if it is a published document, and the year of issue, eg Department of Employment. *Training Employees on the Job*, Cmnd 6354, HMSO, 1991.
- In the case of unpublished documents, the author, the title, what the document is and the year of issue, eg Smith, P.J. *Organisational Dynamics in Multinational Organisations*, PhD Thesis, University of Liverpool, 1989.

There is no 'right' way of presenting this information, so long as it is all there. Look at the acknowledgements sections of other people's reports and at the bibliographies of books, and choose a system that you like. But once you have chosen a system, stick to it and be consistent throughout this section. It will help your readers.

Do you actually want to quote an article or a book in your report? If so you should acknowledge the quote in the text, giving the page reference. So you might put in brackets after a quote: (Smith, p 27). The reader can then refer to your acknowledgements section to find the publication from which it is taken.

### Preparing appendices

Do keep the body of your report as short and as interesting as possible, so that you keep the readers' attention. However, there will be times when you need to provide long documents or tables of figures to support your arguments. These will only clutter up the report and, like acknowledgements, spoil the flow of your argument.

Where you need to provide such documents, therefore, it is a good idea to mention just the main features in the report itself, but reproduce the whole document as an appendix. For example, you might say:

> You may recall that in his report on the new computer systems last year, Jeremy Cornwood concluded that some systems would be better organised on a product rather than a departmental basis (see Appendix A).

You would then reproduce the whole of Jeremy Cornwood's report as Appendix A.

The same principle applies, even when you are not referring to a previously issued document, but to something you have prepared yourself. For example:

> A department-by-department analysis of the company's overheads in the last five years shows a worrying increase in the Systems Department's share in relation to other departments (see Appendix B).

You would then attach your analysis of overheads as Appendix B.

## LAYING OUT TABLES AND CHARTS

No matter how good your command of English, no matter how good you are at writing, there are times when words and figures are not enough. There are times when, to meet the need for clarity, you require a more visual approach. That is when tables and charts come into their own.

When planning to use these devices, however, you will need to choose the right format—the wrong choice will make the information more confused, not less. You should also carefully plan your layout, and how you intend to use your space. Are you going to put them in an appendix or in the text of the report? Both have their advantages and disadvantages.

- If you plan to put charts in the text, you have to allow space for them to be drawn in when the document is being typed. If they are in an appendix, this is not necessary.
- On the other hand, it may be more convenient for your readers to refer to your charts while reading the document, and this will be easier if they are in the text.

### Tables

It is not the purpose of this book to show you how to calculate the figures, percentages, averages etc you may need in your documents, just to show some of the ways in which they can be presented. The easiest and probably the most common way to show figures is to **tabulate** them. How you present your tables will depend on the information you want to convey and its complexity, and in particular what you want to highlight. As an example, let us consider how you might present a comparison between two years' sales figures, broken down into sales areas. At its simplest, such a table might look like figure 39.

| | Year 1 | Year 2 |
|---|---|---|
| | Sales Value | Sales Value |
| UK | £250,000 | £270,000 |
| Europe | £100,000 | £110,000 |
| USA | £100,000 | £100,000 |
| Asia | £30,000 | £40,000 |
| Rest of World | £20,000 | £22,000 |
| TOTAL | £500,000 | £542,000 |

Figure 39. An example of figures presented in a table.

| | Year 1 | | Year 2 | |
|---|---|---|---|---|
| | Sales Value | Profile | Sales Value | Profile |
| UK | £250,000 | 50 | £270,000 | 49.8 |
| Europe | £100,000 | 20 | £110,000 | 20.3 |
| USA | £100,000 | 20 | £100,000 | 18.4 |
| Asia | £30,000 | 6 | £40,000 | 7.4 |
| Rest of World | £20,000 | 4 | £22,000 | 4.1 |
| TOTAL | £500,000 | 100 | £542,000 | 100 |

Figure 40. Figure 39 showing percentage share of the market.

| | Year 1 | | Year 2 | | | | |
|---|---|---|---|---|---|---|---|
| | Sales Value | Prof | Sales Value | Prof | Increase | Inc % | Inc Prof |
| UK | £250,000 | 50 | £270,000 | 49.8 | £20,000 | 8 | 47.6 |
| Europe | £100,000 | 20 | £110,000 | 20.3 | £10,000 | 10 | 23.8 |
| USA | £100,000 | 20 | £100,000 | 18.4 | — | — | |
| Asia | £30,000 | 6 | £40,000 | 7.4 | £10,000 | 33.3 | 23.8 |
| Rest of World | £20,000 | 4 | £22,000 | 4.1 | £2,000 | 10 | 4.7 |
| TOTAL | £500,000 | 100 | £542,000 | 100 | £42,000 | | 100 |

Figure 41. A further extension of figure 39.

This is fine, if that is all the information you want to show. Your readers can see immediately that UK sales increased by £20,000, while Asian sales increased by £10,000. But what if you want to say something about the relative effectiveness of your sales efforts in the two markets? Your readers can probably work out that Asia's £10,000 increase is better than the UK's £20,000. But your job is to make your document easy for them to read: if you want them to make that kind of comparison, you should present your figures in a way that enables them to do so easily. You could for example simply add a column to each of the years, as shown in figure 40. This shows each area's sales as a percentage of the total sales — what is called its profile. Now you can see that UK sales as a proportion of the total actually fell, from 50 to 49.8 per cent, and that Asia's increased, from 6 to 7.4 per cent. This could be vital information when planning future strategies.

That is just another way of showing the same basic information, and again it is fine if that is the picture you want to convey. But sometimes you may not only want to compare actual figures, but perhaps to see how much each segment has contributed to the increase or decrease. Using the figures in figure 39, for example, you know that the UK's sales have increased by £20,000. You also know that total sales have increased by £42,000. But suppose you want to compare the UK's share of that increase (its profile of the increase) with that of say Europe? This is done by adding three more columns to the table, as in figure 41.

Two notes of warning should be sounded at this stage. First, tables should *simplify* your document. *Only* include information which is *relevant*. Do not bore your readers with long tables of figures, only some of which have a bearing on what you are trying to communicate.

Secondly, do make sure that you quote *all* the relevant figures. Do not just use those which prove your point. As Disraeli once said, there are 'lies, damned lies and statistics', and there is no doubt that statistics can be, and often are, used to distort and confuse the facts.

Let us look at an example, using the figures quoted in figures, 39, 40 and 41. If your agent in Asia asks you for an increase in commission, would you argue that he does not deserve it because he has only increased his share of the total market from 6 to 7.4 per cent? Or that he contributed only 23.8 per cent to the year's increase in sales? Superficially, these might seem like good arguments, based on sound statistics. But he has been working from a lower base than other agents, so how could you expect him to have contributed as much to the overall increase? He would be quite justified in pointing out that he has increased sales in his area by 33 per cent—over three times as much as anyone else.

If your figures include averages, make sure that the averages make sense. Do not let unusual items distort them. For example, your company's expenditure in six successive months might be as follows:

| | |
|---|---|
| January | £20,000 |
| February | £18,500 |
| March | £100,000 |
| April | £19,000 |
| May | £17,200 |
| June | £18,000 |
| | |
| Average | £32,117 |

This average bears no relation to any of the monthly figures. It is much higher than most of them, and much lower than March's figure. March was something of an aberration. Perhaps you bought some new machinery or changed a couple of vans, which cost £79,000. It would make far more sense then to take that extraordinary, one-off expenditure out of the average calculation, and to note it separately, as follows:

| | |
|---|---|
| January | £20,000 |
| February | £18,500 |
| March | £21,000 |
| April | £19,000 |
| May | £17,200 |
| June | £18,000 |
| Average | £18,950 |

Note: In March there was a further payment of £79,000 for new machinery, which is not shown in these figures.

## Graphs

There are times when raw information, even in the form of a table, does not make enough of an impact. Since your aim is to make your reader's job easier, you need a way of presenting difficult information in an easily digestible form. Sometimes that form needs to be visual, and the most common form of visual presentation is the graph.

Graphs are used for a variety of purposes, but the most common in business is to show a trend over time. One type of graph is shown in figure 8. The cost of salaries, sales figures, production costs, number of employees, goods produced and overheads are just some of the many statistics than can be plotted graphically to show the underlying trend.

To illustrate this, let us assume that you are a manufacturer. You are taking a long-term look at the costs of your raw materials. Over a six-year period, the cost per item produced is as follows:

| | |
|---|---|
| Year 1: | £3.00 |
| Year 2: | £3.21 |
| Year 3: | £3.50 |
| Year 4: | £3.45 |
| Year 5: | £3.95 |
| Year 6: | £4.27 |

A graph of these figures would look like figure 42. This shows that apart from a dip in year 4, your raw material costs have shown a fairly steady rise. The figures themselves, of course, would show that costs were rising, but the graph brings home how steady the rise is, and what an aberration the year 4 figure is. It might prompt you to investigate the reason for that dip.

You can also compare different sets of figures by plotting two or more lines on the same graph—overheads for different departments,

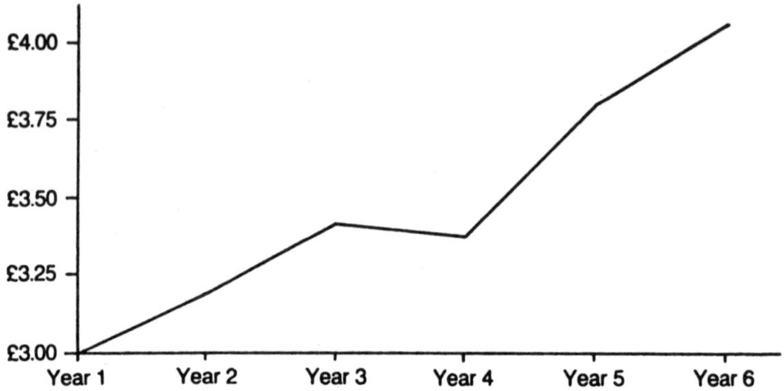


Figure 42. A simple graph showing raw material costs.

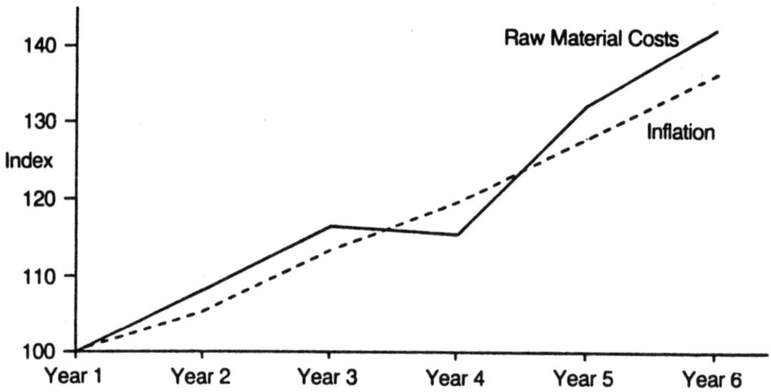


Figure 43. A graph showing raw material costs and inflation.

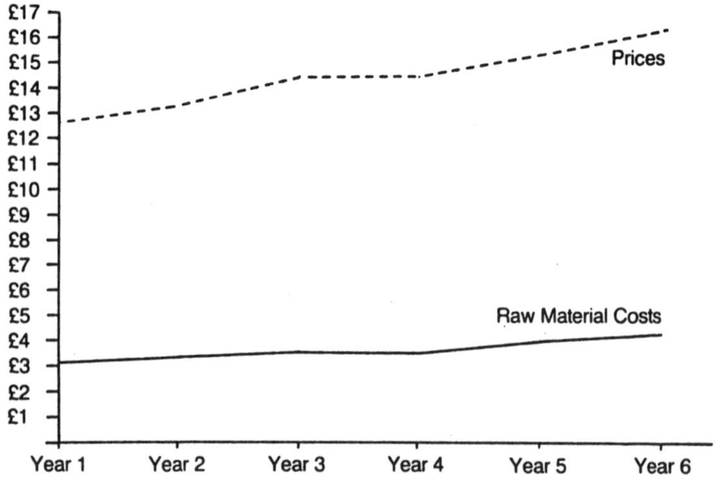


Figure 44. How a graph can be misleading.

for example. You can even compare trends in different fields by using a device called **indexing**. This enables you to compare a trend in, say, overheads (which are expressed in thousands of pounds) with something like the number of employees (expressed as a quantity). It involves giving your first year's figure, whether it is a monetary value, a quantity or a percentage, a value of 100, and relating all subsequent figures to it in proportion. For example, the figures which made up figure 42, expressed as an index, would be:

| | |
|---|---|
| Year 1: | 100 |
| Year 2: | 107 (£3.21 is 1.07 times £3.00) |
| Year 3: | 117 (£3.50 is 1.17 times £3.00) |
| Year 4: | 115 |
| Year 5: | 132 |
| Year 6: | 142 |

The value of indexing can be seen if you want to compare your costs with, say, the rate of inflation. This is a percentage, but it can still be plotted on the same graph. The figures might be:

| | |
|---|---|
| Year 1: | 5% (index 100) |
| Year 2: | 6% (106) |
| Year 3: | 7% (113) |
| Year 4: | 6% (120) |
| Year 5: | 7% (128) |
| Year 6: | 6% (137) |

The comparison in trends can be seen by changing the vertical axis of figure 42 to show index figures, not monetary values, and adding another line, as in figure 43. This shows a rather more disturbing picture, namely that costs are rising at a higher rate than the rate of inflation. It is therefore a trend that might need watching.

You do not have to use indexing, of course. If all the items you want to plot can be expressed in the same terms, you can plot actual values. But will you be comparing like with like, so that your graph makes sense? It would not be very helpful, for example, to plot costs and prices without indexing, even if both are monetary values. In the first place, prices are likely to be so much higher than costs that a slight fluctuation in prices will look much bigger than a similar fluctuation in costs. Look at figure 44, for example. The upward trend in prices looks very much steeper than the trend in costs, because the values are so much higher. In fact, if you look at the individual figures, you will discover that the *percentage* rise in prices is very much *lower* than the rise in costs. As you will see, another problem with this kind of graph is that you end up with a very long vertical axis, with a line at the top for prices and a line at the bottom for costs, which does not help anyone's understanding.

When plotting a graph, always label the axes and show the gradations clearly. If one axis stands for time, always make it the horizontal one.

You can add as many lines to your graph as you like, but do not clutter it, or it will become difficult to interpret. It is best to differentiate the lines with different colours, but if you cannot do that (because you do not have a colour photocopier, for example), then show them as solid and broken lines.

### Bar charts

Graphs are very good for showing trends, but not so good if you want to compare two types of data at a particular time. You can, of course, do this by comparing the points on the graph, but the comparative values are not easily apparent. Look at figure 43, for example: can you immediately see the differences between the rate of inflation and the raw material costs in any one year?

This is where a bar chart comes into its own. You can show a particular year's (or month's) figures for a number of different departments (or activities, or product lines, or countries, or anything else) and have an instant comparison. If you show the figures for more than one period, it will also show you the trend, but not as clearly as a graph.

Here are some statistics showing the overheads of the various departments of a wholesaler's.

| | | |
|---|---|---|
| Year 1: | Sales: | £125,000 |
| | Distribution: | £84,200 |
| | Accounts & Systems: | £126,600 |
| Year 2: | Sales: | £153,500 |
| | Distribution: | £88,500 |
| | Accounts & Systems: | £133,800 |
| Year 3: | Sales: | £181,300 |
| | Distribution: | £93,700 |
| | Accounts & Systems: | £139,400 |

A bar chart of these figures would look like figure 45. As you can see, it is very easy to pick out that in year 1, the Sales Department's overheads were 1½ times those of the Distribution Department, and about the same as those of Accounts and Systems. It is also very easy

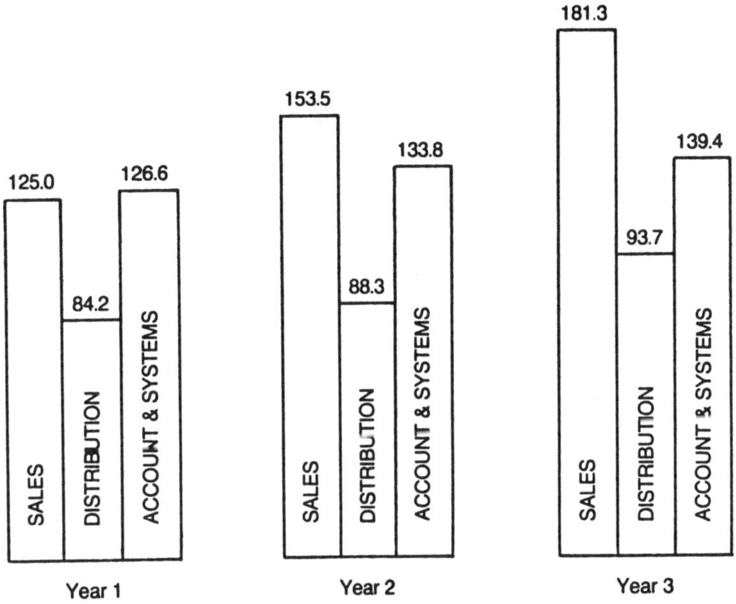


Figure 45. A typical bar chart.

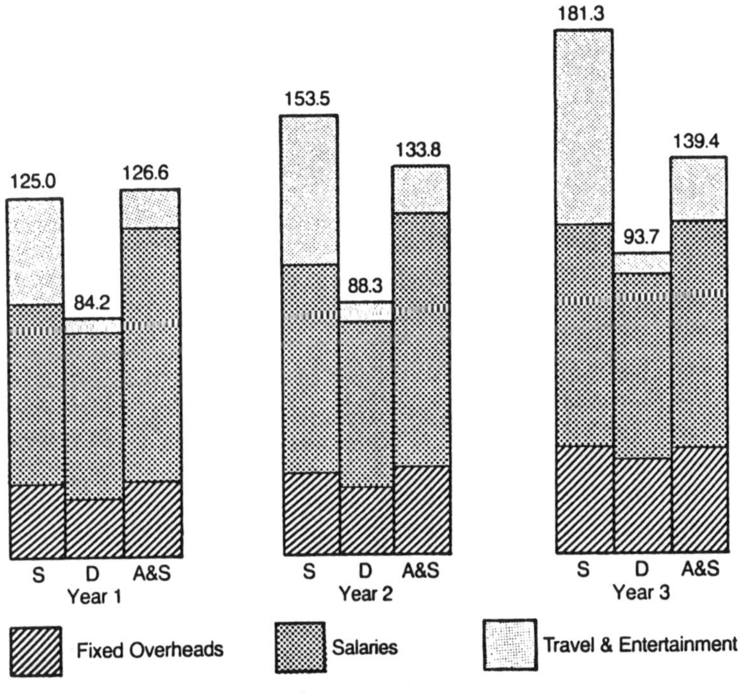


Figure 46. A more detailed bar chart.

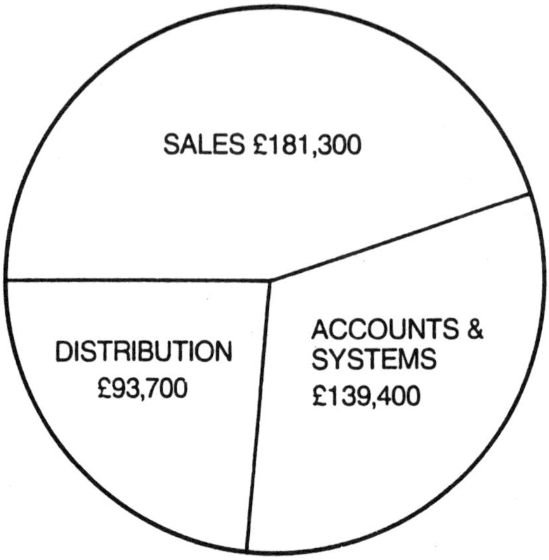


Figure 47. A simple pie chart

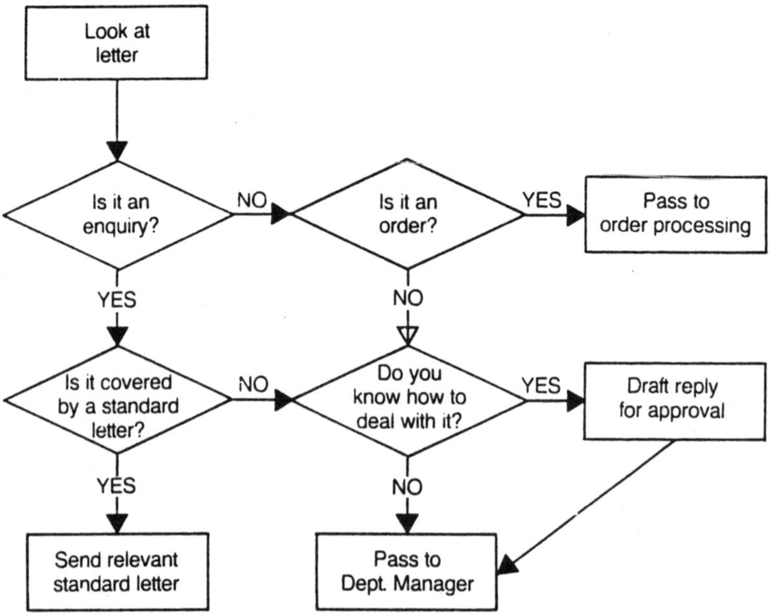


Figure 48. A simple flow chart.

to see that in year 3, they were almost double those for Distribution, and far higher than those for Accounts and Systems. This is very much clearer in a bar chart than it would be in either a table or a graph.

Note that, although the vertical bars are to scale, it is customary to show the actual figures as well, rather than to show a vertical axis with a scale on the left, which would be more difficult to read.

You can make bar charts more sophisticated by subdividing the bars, using different types of shading. So, in our example, you could subdivide each department's bar into different types of overhead, as in figure 46. Now you can see the reason why the Sales Department's overheads have increased by so much more than those of the other departments.

## Pie charts

Pie charts are a good way of showing in what proportions a total figure is split between various sections. The wholesaler's overhead figures, for example, could be presented in this way, as shown in figure 47. Indeed, this would be the best way of presenting them if the aim were to show how the company's overheads were divided between the three departments. But it is not a good way of making comparisons between one set of figures and another. Let us look at figure 47: it shows much more clearly than the bar chart what share of the company's total overheads is allocated to each department. But it is not as easy to see that the Sales Department's overheads are twice as high as Distribution's.

Pie charts can be used for all sorts of figures when you want to show the segmentation of a particular total figure—for example sales figures split into sales areas, total turnover divided between different product lines, or expenditure shown by cost centre. But it is inadvisable to have more than about seven segments, otherwise some of them become so small that they lose their impact. As with bar charts, it is usual to show the actual figures for each segment.

## Flow charts

Flow charts are not used to present figures, but rather to show the flow of work or activity diagrammatically. Again, the aim is to make it easier for your readers to understand what you are saying, and very often a flow chart does this better than a verbal description. Figure 48 shows a simple flow chart for an office dealing with customer enquiries and using standard letters. As you can see, by following the arrows and instructions, it is easy to see what needs to be done at each stage.

Here are a few guidelines to make flowcharts easy to understand and follow.

- The flow should always go from top to bottom and from left to right.
- You should clearly label each activity or decision.
- Use different kinds of box to indicate decisions and actions. In figure 48, actions are represented by rectangles and decisions by lozenges.
- You should show each step in its logical order.
- Use arrows to indicate the direction of the flow.

## CHECKLIST

- Do you use the same style or logo on your letterheads as on your vans and your office?
- Which layout do you prefer in a letter: blocked with open punctuation or indented with full punctuation?
- Do you know the correct way to address your correspondent?
- Does your opening give the reader some idea of what the letter is going to be about, and does it sound interesting?
- Does the body of your letter follow a logical order?
- Does your close indicate to your correspondent what action you expect him or her to take, if any?
- Have you indicated what action you intend to take, if any?
- Are there are special clauses which apply to your business which should be included in your letter?
- If you are writing a report, will the introduction give your readers the background without going into the subject itself?
- Does the body of the report follow a logical sequence?
- Do you need to indicate any conclusions, or should you just highlight your main findings?
- If you are making recommendations, have you given your reasons?
- Is there any long or complex material which you could include as appendices so as not to clutter the body of the report?
- Which method of presenting figures suits your document best—a table, a graph, a bar chart or a pie chart?

# 4
# Writing Sentences and Paragraphs

In any document, it is important to get your **construction** right. No matter how interesting you try to make your subject, no matter how logical your argument is, people will find it difficult to read if it is not well constructed.

The basic building blocks of your document are the words you use; these are built up to form sentences, which in turn are built up to make paragraphs. Here we are concerned with the way you put words together—the sentences you use and how you put them together to form paragraphs.

## WRITING SENTENCES

What is a sentence? According to the dictionary, it is:

- a set of words complete in itself, containing a **subject** and a **predicate**.

There are two terms which need a bit of explanation. The **subject** is the person or thing the sentence is about; it must be a noun, a pronoun or a noun clause, but not a relative pronoun. (If you do not understand these parts of speech, see Chapter 8.) So you cannot say

> I have received your letter. Which points out an error in your account.

The second part of that passage is not a sentence, because there is no subject. The word 'which' is a relative pronoun, which introduces a description of the letter. The passage should read:

> I have received your letter, which points out an error on your account.

The **predicate** tells you something about the subject, and must have a verb. The predicate can describe the subject, or say what it was or did or what was done to it. For example in the sentence

I apologise for the delay

the subject is 'I' (that is who the sentence is about). The predicate is 'apologise for the delay' (that tells us something about the subject – what I am doing). Here is another example:

The cheque is in the post.

Here the subject is 'The cheque' and the predicate is 'is in the post' (it describes the cheque). Sometimes the predicate contains *only* a verb:

The meeting adjourned.

Here the predicate is the verb 'adjourned'.

A common grammatical mistake in business correspondence is to write 'non-sentences' – passages that are used as sentences but do not include both a subject and a predicate. So you cannot say:

Hoping this meets with your approval.

It is not a sentence, as it has no subject – who is hoping? You should say

I hope this meets with your approval.

Now there is a subject: 'I'. The following is also wrong:

There is only one problem. The cost.

Here 'the cost' is not a sentence, as it has no predicate. So the passage should read:

There is only one problem: the cost.

There are two instances where it is permissible to use what look like 'non-sentences': the expression ' thank you', which is short for I thank you'; and requests, invitations,or demands, like ' Please let me know if I can help you.'

A sentence should normally convey a single idea. It can sometimes contain two which are closely connected, but there should never be more than that. If it does contain two ideas, then they must be joined by a conjunction or a relative pronoun (if you do not know what these are, see Chapter 7), or by a semicolon (see Chapter 8). A very common mistake is to writing something like:

I enclose your latest statement, I would like to point that there is an amount of £135 outstanding.

This sentence contains two ideas – the statement and the amount outstanding. They are probably close enough to be included in the same sentence, but they are not joined by a conjunction, a relative pronoun or a semicolon, so the sentence is wrong. It should read:

> I enclose your latest statement, and would like to point out that there is an amount of £135 outstanding.

*or*

> I enclose your latest statement, which I would like to point out shows an amount of £135 outstanding.

*or*

> I enclose your latest statement; I would like to point out that there is an amount of £135 outstanding.

**Types of sentence**

There are four types of sentence, distinguished by their complexity.

*The simple sentence*

It has only one predicate, although it can have more than one subject. It is usually short. Example:

> I have received your letter.

*The compound sentence*

It consists of two or more simple sentences joined by a conjunction:

> I have received your letter and I agree with what you say.

*The complex sentence*

It consists of a main clause and one or more subordinate clauses:

> I have received your letter, which puts your views very clearly.

*The compound complex sentence*

It has two or more main clauses as well as subordinate ones. Example:

> I have received your letter, which puts your views very clearly, and the Manager, to whom I showed it, agrees with what you say.

Because the last three have more than one subject and predicate, they are usually longer. As we will see later, it is better to keep your sentences short, but do not always use simple sentences, even though they are generally shorter. It can be harder for your readers to absorb different simple sentences, all with apparently unconnected bits of information, than to make sense of one long sentence. Figure 49 shows a passage written entirely in simple sentences. You can see how hard it

We must operate as efficiently as possible. I have therefore asked all staff for their ideas on ways to do this. Here are some of those ideas.

We could send all mail by second-class post. This would save us several thousand pounds. It would also make our service worse. We would have to weigh the saving against the loss of customer goodwill.

We could introduce more flexible working practices. Staff could be trained to do several jobs. This would mean that they could be switched to different activities if necessary. For example the order input clerks might be overloaded. In that case some of the accounts clerks could be moved across to help them.

Figure 49. A passage from a memo, using only simple sentences.

Because it is important that we operate as efficiently as possible, I have asked all staff for their ideas on ways to do this. Here are some of those ideas.

We could send all mail by second-class post, which would save us several thousand pounds. However, we would have to weight the saving against the loss of customer goodwill caused by the worsening of service that would result.

We could introduce more flexible working practices. Staff could be trained to do several jobs, so that they could be switched to different activities if necessary. For example, if the order input clerks were overloaded, some of the accounts clerks could be moved across to help them.

Figure 50. A passage from a memo, using a mixture of types of sentence.

is to read, compared with figure 50, which contains sentences of various types.

## Loose and periodic sentence construction

There are also two types of sentence construction: **loose** which has the subject first, as in:

I will circulate a paper before the meeting.

and **Periodic**, which puts subsidiary phrases or clauses before the subject, as in:

> Before the meeting, I will circulate a paper.

As you can see from these examples, loose sentences are more direct; since one of the rules of business correspondence is to be direct, they are to be preferred. However, periodic sentences are useful for building up to your subject, conveying a sense of suspense. They are therefore good for sales letters, where your aim is to hold the readers' attention and make them want to know what is coming next. If you look at figure 63, for example, can you identify the periodic sentences?

Periodic sentences are also useful to make a connection between sentences, and to refer back to the previous sentence. So:

> Can we meet soon? Before the meeting, I will circulate a paper

is better than

> Can we meet soon? I will circulate a paper before the meeting

because 'before the meeting' connects the two sentences by referring back to the first.

### Sentence length

How long should your sentences be? The answer is 'as long as necessary, but no longer'. There is no 'best' length. It all depends on the circumstances. Short sentences generally give a sense of rapid movement and tension, a feeling of urgency. Longer ones are often used in descriptive passages, to develop your argument or perhaps to provide background information. They can given an impression of having been well thought out, and so are good to use from time to time in a report, for example.

Because your aim is to be direct and brief, you should generally *prefer* short sentences, but do not feel that you must *always* use them. As I have said, there are times when longer sentences are more in keeping with what you are trying to convey. It is also good to have a mixture of sentence lengths to avoid monotony and the 'scrappy' appearance of too many short sentences, as you can see by comparing figures 49 and 50.

A sentence should convey a single idea, and it should therefore be as long as is necessary to convey that idea, but no longer.

> The customer's complaint, which concerned the poor quality of our products, should have been dealt with immediately.

It is not particularly long, but it is awkward, because it contains two ideas: the nature of the complaint and the fact that it should have been dealt with. It would be better written like this:

> The customer's complaint concerned the poor quality of our products. It should have been dealt with immediately.

On the other hand, you can get some quite long sentences which are still acceptable since they only convey one idea. It all depends on the idea. For example, the following sentence has one idea, and is short.

> If we promote John Smith, he might not be able to cope with the extra responsibility.

The idea is that John Smith might not be able to cope.

On the other hand, the following sentence, which incorporates the above and is considerably longer, is still acceptable:

> Filling this post presents a problem, because if we appoint from outside, we increase our workforce at a time when we should be cutting back; whereas if we promote John Smith, he might not be able to cope with the extra responsibility.

There is still only one idea, but this time it is that filling the post is a problem. The clause about John Smith only qualifies it.

### Avoiding awkward sentences

There are several ways in which your sentences can become clumsy and awkward. Sometimes this is because they are incorrect grammatically, but even sentences which are quite correct can sometimes sound wrong. The most common causes of clumsy sentences are:

- incorporating two ideas in one sentence;
- putting too many subsidiary clauses before the subject in a periodic sentence;
- leaving 'hanging participles';
- letting a sentence get 'out of parallel'.

We have already seen the awkward results of putting more than one idea in one sentence, and the more ideas you try to incorporate, the more unwieldy it becomes. Look at the following sentence, for example:

> I am afraid that we are out of stock of that item and are not expecting new stocks for four weeks, at which time we will

> supply your order unless you decide that you would prefer to cancel, in which case I would be grateful if you could let me know.

This is far too long and unwieldy, and incorporates three ideas:

1. That you are out of stock for four weeks.
2. That you will supply the customer's order when the stocks arrive, unless they cancel.
3. That if they do cancel, you would like them to let you know.

So the passage should be rewritten in three sentences:

> I am afraid that we are out of stock of that item and are not expecting new stocks for four weeks. As soon as they arrive, we will supply your order, unless you decide that you would prefer to cancel. If you do decide to cancel, I would be grateful if you could let me know.

As we have seen, periodic sentences can be useful for building up to a subject, and keeping the reader's interest. But carried too far, they can simply become unwieldy, as the following sentence shows:

> When I came to the end of my familiarisation exercise, having spent eight weeks looking in great detail at the way we operate at all levels, during which time I visited all our branches and spoke to most of our staff at all levels, I felt that I knew the company intimately.

There is nothing wrong with this sentence grammatically, but it is awkward to read because it takes too long to get to the main clause 'I felt that I knew the company intimately'. The reader will probably be bored to tears by the time he or she gets there.

**Hanging participles** are those which start adjectival phrases that have become separated from the nouns they qualify. Can you see what is wrong with the following sentence?

> Our February statement has not yet been attended to, showing an outstanding balance of £3,560.

The problem is that 'showing an outstanding balance of £3,560' is an adjectival phrase which is meant to qualify 'our February statement'. But because the two phrases have been separated, it looks awkward—you are left wondering what 'showing an outstanding balance of £3,560' refers to. The participle 'showing' is therefore said to be

Seaview Hotel
Marine Parade
Portstown
HG15 3GF
Tel. (0987) 23876

Mr Dipak Patel
Sales Manager
Green & Sons plc
53 Hilton Road
Portstown
HG15 2FW

Our ref. GHS/HJ/23
5 May 1994

Dear Mr Patel

Following our telephone conversation last week, I would like to confirm the arrangements for your sales conference on 15 and 16 May. We have reserved the small conference room for you. This seats forty people, and since there will only be thirty attending there will be plenty of room for everyone. We will provide seating and tables in a rectangular layout, as you requested. We will also provide a flip pad and easel and an overhead projector. If you also need video facilities, they will be available, and you need only ask me on the day. We will serve lunch on both days, in a separate room. Menus are attached. I understand that only the wine with the meal is to be charged to your company, and that any other drinks should be paid for. A private bar will be set aside for your use. I have also reserved fifteen rooms with private baths for those who are staying overnight. I look forward to seeing you on the 15th, and thank you for choosing our hotel for your venue.

Yours sincerely

Geraldine Summers
Conference Manager

Figure 51. A letter with only one paragraph.

hanging. The sentence should read:

> Our February statement, showing an outstanding balance of £3,560, has not yet been attended to.

Keeping your sentence **in parallel** means ensuring that you do not combine two different parts of speech in the same construction. It is wrong, for example, to say:

> The meeting was chaotic and a disaster.

'Chaotic' is an adjective and 'a disaster' is a noun, so the sentence looks clumsy. They must both be one or the other. So it should read:

> The meeting was chaotic and disastrous.

Now they are both adjectives and the sentence is in parallel.

The same rule applies to different forms of the verb. For example, the following is wrong:

> Our aims are to reduce costs and serving our customers.

'To reduce' is an infinitive, and 'serving' is a participle. They should both be one or the other. So you can *either* say:

> Our aims are **to reduce** costs and **to serve** our customers.

*or*

> Our aims are **reducing** costs and **serving** our customers.

Do not worry about the terms 'infinitive' and 'participle'. Just think of them as the 'to' form and the '-ing' form; remember that you must use one or the other but not both, and you will be all right.

### Changing your emphasis in a sentence

You can change the emphasis of your sentences simply by changing the order of the words. The parts of a sentence that most people remember are the beginning and the end. So any points you want to emphasise should go there. Consider the following example:

> I notified you three weeks ago that I had received the wrong consignment, and to date I have had no response.

Here the emphasis is on the notification. But you could change the order, to read:

> Three weeks ago, I notified you that I had received the wrong consignment, and to date I have received no response.

Now the emphasis is on the fact that it was three weeks ago that you notified them. You can add even more emphasis by using 'it was'. This turns a phrase into a clause and gives it more stress. So the above sentence could read:

> It was three weeks ago that I notified you that I had received the wrong consignment, and to date I have received no response.

This is even stronger than the above example.

Seaview Hotel
Marine Parade
Portstown
HG15 3GF
Tel. (0987) 23876

Mr Dipak Patel
Sales Manager
Green & Sons plc
53 Hilton Road
Portstown
HG15 2FW

Our ref. GHS/HJ/23
5 May 1995

Dear Mr Patel

Following our telephone conversation last week, I would like to confirm the arrangements for your sales conference on 15 and 16 May.

We have reserved the small conference room for you. This seats forty people, and since there will only be thirty attending there will be plenty of room for everyone. We will provide seating and tables in a rectangular layout, as you requested. We will also provide a flip pad and easel and an overhead projector. If you also need video facilities, they will be available, and you need only ask me on the day.

We will serve lunch on both days, in a separate room. Menus are attached. I understand that only the wine with the meal is to be charged to your company, and that any other drinks should be paid for. A private bar will be set aside for your use.

I have also reserved fifteen rooms with private baths for those who are staying overnight.

I look forward to seeing you on the 15th, and thank you for choosing our hotel for your venue.

Yours sincerely

Geraldine Summers
Conference Manager

Figure 52. A letter with proper paragraphing.

## WRITING PARAGRAPHS

Just as a sentence should deal with a single idea, or two closely related ideas joined by a connecting word, so a paragraph should deal with just one collection of ideas, one theme or topic. Just as a sentence can become awkward and unwieldy if too many ideas are introduced, so a paragraph will be difficult to follow if there are two many topics competing for the reader's attention; the brain has to store a number of different ideas before it can start working on one of them. It also looks difficult to read, so the reader is almost subconsciously put off before he or she even starts. Look at the letter in figure 51. It is not easy to distinguish one thought from another, and reading it is hard work. Now look at the new version in figure 52. Is it not easier to read? Yet all that has been done is to divide it into separate paragraphs.

It follows from this that you should start a new paragraph with each new topic. But you can also use paragraphing to indicate that you are about to look at the same topic, but from a different angle, as the following extract shows:

> I can offer you a complete service — not just office cleaning, but also laundry and towel replacement. I will even look after your reception area for you, ensuring that your plants are cared for and that there is an attractive collection of magazines available.
>
> Of course, if all you want is an office cleaning service, I can provide that on its own, and I think you will find my rates and my service the best in town.

The first paragraph deals with the services you offer. The second also deals with those services, so it is in fact covering the same topic. But it covers it from a different angle—the angle of the customer who does not want a complete service.

You can also use paragraphing to develop your topic, or an element or concept within it, as in the following:

> For all these reasons, our strategy must be one of expansion. We do not yet fully exploit our potential in the market, and there are many areas where there is room to improve our performance. The most important, and potentially the most profitable, of these is the export market.
>
> Exports account for only 15 per cent of total sales. With careful planning, the right personnel and a certain amount of investment, we could increase that to 25 per cent within a year.

Here, you are continuing with the same topic, but you are developing an element of it (exports) until it becomes a topic in its own right.

Many people, when planning their documents, actually list the paragraph topics so that they know what is to go into each paragraph. It can be a very useful technique, especially if you use the listing method of outlining. You can then develop a paragraph out of each of the points on your list.

## Paragraph length

Short paragraphs are preferable to long ones. As you can see in figures

51 and 52, shorter paragraphs *look* easier to read; if your reader *thinks* that your document is going to be easy to read, then the battle is half won. If, on the other hand, you have very long paragraphs, your document looks boring and you will have an uphill task convincing your reader that it is not.

Very short, single-sentence paragraphs can be used for emphasis. They tend to bring your readers up short, to make them sit up and take notice. Look at the following passage:

> I spoke to you on the telephone on 16 January. You said that there had been problems with your bank, and promised that payment would be made by 20 January.
>
> It was not.
>
> I telephoned you again on 25 January, but you were not available. Your assistant told me that there was a cheque in the post, and that it would be with me the following day.
>
> It was not.

Can you see how useful the single-sentence paragraphs are for emphasising the fact that payment has not been received? The repetition is particularly effective in hammering home the message. But use this device sparingly. Its effectiveness lies in the fact that it is unusual. If you use it too much, it loses its 'shock' value, and your documents will just look disjointed.

As with sentences, it pays to vary the length of your paragraphs to lend variety to your writing. A document consisting solely of short paragraphs will be almost as hard to read as one with only long paragraphs. Much will depend, of course, on the topics you are discussing; if you find that you have a number of very short paragraphs, check to see whether they really do each cover a complete topic.

A lot will also depend on the document. Paragraphs in a report will usually be longer than those in a letter or a memo, because a report is usually longer, and the subject is usually discussed at greater length.

### The topic sentence

Each paragraph should have a topic sentence, one which encapsulates what the paragraph is going to be about. This should be at the beginning of the paragraph, usually the first sentence. Look at some of the examples above and at figure 52, and you will see the topic sentences:

> 'I can offer you a complete service...' tells you that the paragraph is going to be about your service.
>
> 'Exports account for only 15 per cent of total sales' tells you that the paragraph is going to be about exports.
>
> 'I spoke to you on the telephone...' tells you that the paragraph is going to be about the telephone conversation.
>
> 'We have reserved the small conference room...' tells you that the paragraph is going to be about the conference room.
>
> 'We will serve lunch on both days' tells you that the paragraph is going to be about the lunch arrangements.

The advantage of topic sentences is that they make it easier to follow the flow of your document by telling the reader what to expect from each paragraph. They might even be based on the points in your list outline.

### Expanding your theme

The topic sentence introduces the paragraph, but you need to expand from that basic idea into a full paragraph. There are several techniques for this, depending on what you want to say. These are the most common.

*1. Arguing your case*

You might make a statement in your topic sentence and then explain it in the rest of the paragraph. For example:

> We must be totally confident that you will be able to meet our deadline. It is extremely costly to have our machines lying idle. It is not only a question of having to pay operators when there is no work to be done, but the shut-down and start-up costs are extremely high.

The topic sentence makes the statement, and the rest of the paragraph sets out the arguments why the deadline must be set.

*2. Presenting the background*

Your topic sentence might outline the subject of the paragraph, with the rest of the paragraph providing the background information:

> Nigeria is one of our most important sales areas. With a population estimated at around 100 million, it represents a huge market, and one which we have not yet fully tapped. It is a

> country of entrepreneurs, with a thirst for consumer goods. Although it has been through several phases of upheaval, it is at present reasonably stable.

The topic sentence signals that the paragraph is going to be about Nigeria as a sales area, and the rest of the paragraph expands on the topic by giving further information about Nigeria.

*3. Reinforcing your message*

You might use your paragraph to reinforce the point made in your topic sentence by repeating it from a different perspective:

> Our costs are rising at a worrying rate. Raw material prices increased by 15 per cent this year. Overheads increased by 20 per cent, partly because of an increase in our rent. And payroll costs increased by 10 per cent, even though we actually saw a fall in the number of staff.

Here the second, third and fourth sentences give examples of the way costs have risen, thus emphasising the message of the topic sentence.

*4. Outlining the consequences*

You might make a statement in your topic sentence and then use the rest of the paragraph to show what the results might be:

> We have not met our turnover budget this year. This means that we will have to reduce our overheads substantially next year. Redundancies will be inevitable.

*5. Giving your reasons*

You might outline a situation in your topic sentence, and then give the reasons for that situation in the rest of the paragraph:

> I am afraid that we are not able to supply your order at present. The reason is that there has been an industrial dispute at the factory which manufactures these items. We are trying to locate another source of supply, but have been unable to do so yet.

These are only the most common techniques for expanding your paragraph, and they are given here as suggestions only. Do not feel that you *must* use them. There may be situations which you feel do not fit any of these techniques. In that case, develop your paragraph in the way you think suits the situation best. As long as the information is presented in a logical way, it does not matter a great deal what technique you use.

### Paragraph headings

Whether you use headings for your paragraphs is largely a matter of personal preference, but when deciding whether to use them or not, bear the following in mind:

- Headings usually interrupt the flow of the text, so they should only be used where they serve a genuine purpose.
- They can often be useful to the reader 'skimming' your document, as they will give a quick idea of its contents.
- The are usually inappropriate for short documents, like most letters and memos, where the reader can get a good idea of the contents by reading the whole thing. In these cases they simply interfere with the flow.
- They can make a complex document easier to read by highlighting the main points.
- They make cross-referencing easier.

### Getting the flow right

We have seen how you can expand your paragraph by developing the subject of your topic sentence logically. The same goes for the development of your document as a whole. It should flow logically, one topic leading on to the next. Conduct your reader through it without jumping from subject to subject. Each paragraph should have a natural connection with the previous one.

There are two ways of making this connection:

- By taking an idea from the last sentence of one paragraph, and using it to start the next.
- By using various forms of words to signal the direction your argument or narrative is going to take.

Let us look at each of these in more detail.

Repeating an idea from one paragraph at the beginning of the next creates a very smooth flow to your document. There is a clear link and the reader can follow you very easily. Look at this passage:

> At Sunnyside Garden Centre we pride ourselves on being able to satisfy even the most demanding of customers. That is why we carry the widest range of tools in the area.
>
> We have something for every job, from powerful motor mowers to simple trowels.

**SUNNYSIDE GARDEN CENTRE**

Oak Tree Cross
Towerbridge Road
King's Beech
LT21 4SK

27 March 1995

Dear Customer

Spring is on its way, and with it the chance to get out and enjoy your garden. Whether you have a large allotment or just a patio, now is the time to start sowing and planting so as to get the most out of it later in the year.

Your garden will certainly need digging, composting and fertilising in preparation for the growing season.

Why not come down to Sunnyside Garden Centre? We have plants and seeds galore, from fruit trees to phlox seeds and from artichokes to amaryllis, together with every conceivable medium to grow them in. And if you aren't sure of the best varieties for your needs, you only have to ask. Many of our staff are experts in various fields.

We can give you a complete service, whatever your needs. We have sprays to control pests and diseases you didn't even know existed, a complete range of organic products and the widest range of tools in the area.

Any new product we stock is tested by our staff before we sell it, so that we can personally recommend everything on our shelves.

We pride ourselves on being able to satisfy even the most demanding of customers. Our motto is 'Try harder', and we do. Our staff are friendly and helpful, but never pushy.

We haven't forgotten the children. We have just opened a new section devoted entirely to slides, swings, climbing frames and other equipment to make your garden fun to be in, whatever your age.

Why not pay us a visit? We look forward to seeing you soon.

Yours sincerely

Jack Kemp
Managing Director

Figure 53. A letter without any links between paragraphs.

Can you see how the idea of the wide range of equipment is repeated in the first sentence of the second paragraph, thus creating a smooth transition from one paragraph to the next?

You can make the repetition even more direct, by repeating one of the words in the previous sentence, or by replacing it with a pronoun or a **synonym** (a word with a similar meaning). So the second paragraph in the above passage could have begun with

We have tools for every job
We have them for every job
We have equipment for every job

Very often, however, the new paragraph cannot be introduced simply by repeating an idea from the previous one. You may be about to change direction, or look at the same topic from a different angle. But you still need to make a link with what has gone before. So you can use different expressions to show where you are going. Which particular one you use depends on what purpose the new paragraph serves, but here are a few examples:

The reason is...
You will understand that...
This means that...
For example...
Indeed...
What is more...

All of these tell the reader that you are going to expand on what has gone before, or explain it more fully.

However...
Even so...
Nevertheless...
On the other hand...

These show that you are changing direction.

Therefore...
Similarly...
As a result...

These indicate that you are moving forward, going on to the next stage of the discussion.

Finally...
To summarise...

## SUNNYSIDE GARDEN CENTRE

Oak Tree Cross
Towerbridge Road
King's Beech
LT21 4SK

27 March 1991

Dear Customer

Spring is on its way, and with it the chance to get out and enjoy your garden. Whether you have a large allotment or just a patio, now is the time to start sowing and planting so as to get the most out of it later in the year.

And it is not only sowing and planting you should be thinking of. Your garden will certainly need digging, composting and fertilising in preparation for the growing season.

So why not come down to Sunnyside Garden Centre? We have plants and seeds galore, from fruit trees to phlox seeds and from artichokes to amaryllis, together with every conceivable medium to grow them in. And if you aren't sure of the best varieties for your needs, you only have to ask. Many of our staff are experts in various fields.

What this means is that we can give you a complete service, whatever your needs. We have sprays to control pests and diseases you didn't even know existed, a complete range of organic products and the widest range of tools in the area.

We have equipment for every job, from motor mowers to simple trowels. Any new product we stock is tested by our staff before we sell it, so that we can personally recommend everything on our shelves.

What is more, we pride ourselves on being able to satisfy even the most demanding of customers. Our motto is 'Try harder', and we do. Our staff are friendly and helpful, but never pushy.

Finally, we haven't forgotten the children. We have just opened a new section devoted entirely to slides, swings, climbing frames and other equipment to make your garden fun to be in, whatever your age.

So why not pay us a visit? We look forward to seeing you soon.

Yours sincerely

Jack Kemp
Managing Director

Figure 54. A letter with various linking devices to make it flow smoothly.

These indicate that this is the last paragraph in your document, and that you are bringing it to a neat close.

Figure 53 shows a sales letter from the Sunnyside Garden Centre. Can you see how disjointed it looks? But the same letter, with just the linking devices added, as in figure 54, flows quite smoothly. The devices used are:

1. 'And it is not only sowing and planting...'—repetition combined with the expression 'not only' to indicate that the writer is going to expand on this subject.
2. 'So why not come down...?'—'so' shows that he is going on to the next stage.
3. 'What this means is...'—he is going to explain further.
4. 'We have equipment...'—repetition of the idea from the last sentence of the previous paragraph.
5. 'What is more' — again he is going to expand on his subject.
6. 'Finally, we haven't forgotten...'—'finally' indicates that this is the concluding paragraph.

## CHECKLIST

- Does your correspondence contain a variety of types and lengths of sentence?
- Which have you used most: short and simple sentences or long and complex or compound ones?
- Which kind of construction is best for your particular document – loose or periodic?
- Are your sentences in parallel?
- Are there any hanging participles?
- Are your sentences constructed so as to put the emphasis where you want it?
- Are your paragraphs short enough, and of varied length?
- Does each paragraph have a topic sentence, and develop the topic logically?
- Are headings appropriate for your document?
- Have you used the right techniques and expressions to link your paragraphs logically?

# 5
# Achieving Good Business Style

So far we have discussed the 'mechanics' of business correspondence—how to plan your document, how to set it out, how to construct it. We now come to the content—what you want to say and how you are going to say it, in other words your style.

There are two elements to style in writing: the **tone** you use and the **words** you use. Both are important in giving your document the right quality and in achieving the reaction you want.

## USING THE RIGHT TONE

Although the tone of your letter partly depends on which words you use, it also depends on how you use them. If you set out to be friendly, for example, you will express yourself in a way which gives that 'feel' to your letter. If you are not pleased about something, you will choose forms of expression which make that clear, just as you do when you are speaking.

### Be sincere

One of the most important things to remember in getting your tone right is to be sincere. Whether you are writing a sales letter, replying to an enquiry or making a complaint, you must believe in what you are saying, and that belief must come through into your writing. So think before you write something: do you really mean it? And when you have written it, read it through and see whether you *sound* as though you mean it. Look at the following passage:

> We acknowledge with thanks receipt of your recent communication, and enclose a copy of our catalogue as requested. Should you have any queries, the undersigned will be pleased to assist you.

Reading this, do you get the feeling that the 'undersigned' really *will* be pleased to assist you? It does not much sound like it, does it? The language is so stiff and formal that it becomes merely a form of words, without real meaning.

Now look at the next passage.

> I would like to thank you most sincerely for taking the time to write to us, and for giving us the opportunity to serve you. Here is your very own personal copy of our catalogue, to browse through at your leisure. If you have any queries, I would love to help you. I'll be waiting for your call.

This writer goes too far in the other direction. The tone is too gushing, too good to be true. First, if you are being sincere, the last thing you want to do is *say* so. If you have to tell people that you are being sincere, then you have failed in getting your sincerity across in your writing. Secondly, do you really believe that someone is sitting there, just waiting for your call? And is there anything special about having your 'very own personal copy' of a catalogue rather than just a 'copy'?

Now see how you can say the same thing simply, straightforwardly and yet with sincerity.

> Thank you for your letter. I am pleased to enclose our latest catalogue, for you to browse through at your leisure. If you have any queries, I would be happy to help, so just give me a ring.

This letter is not over-formal, but nor does it gush. It does not give the impression that the writer is merely using a form of words because it is the 'done' thing, but it also does not sound as though he or she is trying too hard. In other words, it sounds sincere.

### Be clear

Your document should be as clear, as precise and as direct as possible. Your tone, the way you use your words and sentences, can usually help to achieve this. Test your writing for clarity with this questionnaire.

1. If a particular point is unusual or especially important, have you tried to emphasise it by expounding on it at length? This is the wrong way to create emphasis. It's much better to use short, one-sentence paragraphs, repeat the word or the idea once or twice in short sentences, or even use underlining or block capitals if necessary. But do not become bogged down in long explanations. That will have the opposite effect.

2. Have you used any vague expressions? You should not, for example, use terms like 'a significant increase'. How big is significant? It could mean almost anything. If you know the

amount of the increase, then state it. If not then just say 'an increase'.

3. Have you used any euphemisms? At best euphemisms use more words than a direct statement and at worst they can be misunderstood. Don't say 'Profits showed a negative trend' when you mean 'We made a loss', or even when you mean 'Profits were down on last year'. Not only does it sound as though you are trying to hide something, but as we have just seen, it could mean either of two things.
4. Can any of your words be understood more than one way? If you use the word 'sales', for example, is it clear whether you mean sales volume or sales value? And can your readers tell whether an expression like 'improvement in profitability' means increased profits or higher profit margins?
5. Can any of your sentences be understood in more than one way? For example, do not say 'I need to know what our costs will be by the end of the month' if you mean 'I need to know by the end of the month what our costs will be.' The two sentences mean two different things.
6. Do you give all the information required? For example, if you are giving a quotation, have you
   (a) *precisely* described the goods or services for which you are quoting;
   (b) given the prices and the cost of any extras;
   (c) given the delivery date, if appropriate?

### Be brief

As discussed in Chapter 1, one of the cardinal rules in business communications is brevity. Business people do not want to waste time reading through pages of superfluous verbiage. They want information, but they want to be able to absorb it as quickly as possible.

One way of achieving brevity, of course is to use as few words as you can. You should not, however, let brevity get in the way of clarity. If shortening your document makes it incomplete or difficult to follow, then leave it as it is. Nor should you choose brevity before politeness. If using fewer words means omitting some of the courtesies, it is not worth it.

There are three main causes of wordiness in business communications:

- circumlocution

- vague qualifiers
- padding

*Circumlocution*
This means using a long expression when a short one will do. For example, do not say 'I have caused enquiries to be made with a view to establishing the reasons for our inability to supply your order.' This can be said quite simply, in fewer than half the words: 'I have enquired into the reasons why we were not able to supply your order.' Some people think that circumlocution adds weight to their correspondence. It does not. All it does is make it sound pompous, and add to the length.

*Vague qualifiers*
These are adjectives and adverbs that do not mean anything. These include 'really', 'good', 'nice' and various other words which are usually used because the writer cannot be bothered to think of anything more precise or simply because they are handy 'fillers'. What, for example, is a 'really productive meeting'? How much more productive is it than just a 'productive meeting'? Is it as productive as a 'very productive meeting'? Is a 'good' candidate someone who interviews well, someone who is suitable for the job, someone with the right qualifications, or all three?

*Padding*
This means expressions which serve no useful purpose, but which just fill the document. These include expressions like 'It should be noted that...' and 'I must say that...' But beware. Although most such expressions are unnecessary, some can serve a useful purpose. For example, 'You will appreciate that...' sounds like padding, but it can be used to get the reader on your side. For example, if you want to explain why you are unable to give a customer a higher discount, you can say:

> You will appreciate that our discounts are already generous. Our margins are therefore already tight, and any increase in discount would erode them yet further.

This appeals to your customer as a reasonable and intelligent person who will understand these problems.

### Achieving a conversational tone
There was a time when all business correspondence was expected to be

CARSTAIRS CLOTHING COMPANY
43 Gorton Road, Marsby, MB2 4HY
Tel. (01921) 143267 (24 hours)

Our ref: CP/TS

26 August 1994

Mrs A. Maxwell
13 Thrixton Crescent
Charterborough
LT14 6TU

Dear Madam

We are in receipt of your letter of 15 August regarding the return of a dress, item number 456732. On investigation, it appears that the dress was indeed received. Your account has therefore been credited with the appropriate amount.

We are only able to entertain claims for compensation if actual financial loss has been incurred. This is quite obviously not the case in this instance.

Yours faithfully

Catherine Porter
Customer Relations Manager

Figure 55. A formal, unfriendly letter.

formal and impersonal. That is no longer the case. Look at figure 55. Would you like to receive such a letter? How would *you* react to the person who wrote it? You probably would not even relate to her as a person. It is strange how many people still send letters like this, even though they probably complain bitterly about impersonal business people when they receive one.

Letters like this now look at best old fashioned, and at worst almost rude. People do not speak like that, so why should you write like that? Of course, you could not write exactly as you speak, as we saw in Chapter 1—for one thing, you are expected to follow the rules of grammar in your writing. But if you get close to a conversational tone, your document will sound friendlier and be more likely to achieve the reaction you want. So how can it be improved?

1. Catherine Porter could address Mrs Maxwell as 'Dear Mrs Maxwell', rather than 'Dear Madam' (see **The salutation** in Chapter 3).
2. She could use 'I' rather than 'we'. 'We' is a way of hiding behind your company, avoiding responsibility. You should only use it if you really mean the company as a whole.
3. She could replace formal expressions like 'We acknowledge receipt' with more informal ones.
4. She could use the active rather than the passive voice. 'I have credited your account' rather than 'Your account has been credited'. The first sounds friendlier, the second is very impersonal.
5. She could be more apologetic about the company's error. Nothing is more annoying that receiving a letter in which the company admits to having made a mistake but does not bother to apologise.
6. She could be more tactful in turning down Mrs Maxwell's request for compensation. There is no reason not to be firm if the situation calls for it, but you can be firm *and* friendly.

Figure 56 shows the same letter written in a friendlier, more conversational way. Which would *you* prefer to receive? When you are doing your own writing, try to think how you would feel if the communication were addressed to you. The more conversational tone is usually much better.

### The right tone for your purposes

We need to adopt different tones of voice for different kinds of communication, just as we do in speech. So, for example, a letter apologising for an error needs to be apologetic and conciliatory, a sales letter enthusiastic, a letter demanding payment forceful. The key to achieving the right tone is to think of the reaction you want, and to adopt the most appropriate tone.

Not only will your tone change according to the nature of your document, it will also be different for different readers. So, for example, you may ask yourself 'Who is in charge?' If you are asking a

CARSTAIRS CLOTHING COMPANY

43 Gorton Road, Marsby, MB2 4HY
Tel. (01921) 143267 (24 hours)

Our ref: CP/TS

26 August 1994

Mrs A. Maxwell
13 Thrixton Crescent
Charterborough
LT14 6TU

Dear Mrs Maxwell

I was very sorry to see from your letter of 15 August that you are still being charged for a dress which you returned to us. I have investigated the matter, and it appears that we did indeed receive it, but that owing to an error in our Accounts Department, your account was not adjusted. I do apologise for this oversight, and for the inconvenience you have been caused. I have now credited your account with £55.75.

I am afraid, however, that I cannot give you any financial compensation. We are always happy to consider claims for compensation when there has been some financial loss as a result of our error, but as I understand it, you have not suffered any such loss.

I am sorry you have had to write to us about this matter, and I hope you understand our position on the question of compensation.

Yours sincerely

Catherine Porter
Customer Relations Manager

Figure 56. A less formal, friendly and apologetic letter.

favour, your tone will not be the same as it will if you are making a demand. For example, you might write a memo to your Managing Director as follows:

> I wonder whether you would agree to the company paying something towards the staff's Christmas party this year.

You might, on the other hand, write as follows to a supplier who has made an error.

> This is the third time I have had to write to you about this matter. I am afraid that if I do not receive a satisfactory reply within the next week, I shall be forced to take the necessary legal action.

No matter what you are writing, however, and no matter who it is addressed to, you should always be polite. You can make your point clearly, but never be rude. Even if you are in charge, you still want something from your reader, and politeness is more likely to get it than rudeness. And if you are a manager, it is not only unproductive but also extremely unfair to be rude to your subordinates, as they cannot answer you in kind.

Rudeness often goes hand in hand with emotion, and you should never be emotional in business writing. Argue your case forcefully by all means, show your displeasure if you need to, but do not let emotion dictate the tone of your document. You are very unlikely to get the reaction you want.

It is a good idea, when you sit down to plan your document, to think of both the positive and the negative sides of what you are about to say, and to emphasise the positive while playing down or trying to ameliorate the negative. In this way, you will have a document which comes over as positive, whatever your message.

This applies even to something like a letter making a final demand for payment. Look at the letter in figure 57. It is as firm as it needs to be, and Lionel Grantham does not mince his words. He sets out quite clearly the consequences of non-payment. But while doing this, he emphasises the positive side of paying (Harold Mills will avoid the embarrassment of being taken to court). The result is a positive, polite, yet forceful letter, which is far more likely to achieve the result Lionel wants than a rude, negative one. Lionel may have felt like writing an extremely rude letter after waiting so long for payment but he was wise to curb his annoyance.

This idea of emphasising the positive side of what you have to say applies whatever kind of communication you are writing. For example, if you have reorganised your company and are writing to tell your clients, do not just say:

> I am writing to tell you about some changes we have made.

If you say:

> We have made some changes in our organisation which will, I am sure, improve our service to you

then you introduce a positive element which makes a favourable impression on the recipient.

ABC OFFICE EQUIPMENT
54 Union Street
Kingston St Mary
GY14 6FD
Tel. 01321 908743

16 November 1994

Mr Harold Mills
Financial Director
NWS Manufacturing
NWS House
Kingston St Mary
GY14 7TP

Dear Mr Mills

I am very sorry to see that, despite my letters of 31 August, 15 September and 30 September, as well as a number of telephone calls, we have still not been paid the amount outstanding on your account. Perhaps I could remind you that the sum concerned is £600.75, and that it has been outstanding since June.

Our normal policy when payment has been overdue for so long without any reason being offered is to pursue our claim through the courts. I am sure that you would not want the embarrassment and publicity that that would entail, and we for our part would be sorry to have to take that kind of action against a company which has been a valued customer for a long time. We are therefore prepared to delay any action for one week more. If we receive payment within that time, then we can both be spared the unpleasantness of legal action.

I look forward to receiving your cheque.

Yours sincerely

Lionel Grantham
Credit Controller

Figure 57. An extremely firm but still polite letter.

## CHOOSING THE RIGHT WORDS

When choosing your words, bear in mind the rules of business correspondence: brevity, clarity and directness. Use words that help achieve these aims. The secret is to keep it simple. The average person knows about 5,000 words, and probably uses 3,000. But we do not all use the same 3,000, so the more complex your words become, the more likely you are to be using words with which your readers are unfamiliar. For example, use the word ‘use’ rather than ‘utilise’, ‘buy’ rather than 'purchase', and 'try' rather than 'endeavour'. And *never* use a word unless you are sure you know exactly what it means.

I have a test which I use when I am writing. If I look at a sentence and think, 'That looks impressive', then I know that I have used long words that could be replaced by simpler ones. The main reason why people use long, complex words is that they think they look impressive. Do not be tempted; they are not impressive, just long-winded.

There are three common faults which will make your document long-winded, and which should therefore be avoided:

- jargon
- tautology
- unnecessary abstract nouns

There are another three faults which will make it look sloppy, and these too should be avoided:

- clichés
- slang
- abbreviations

### Avoiding jargon

Jargon is technical language which is specific to a group or profession. Sometimes it is necessary, especially in the scientific and technical fields. Even in business writing, there may be times when you need to use a technical term which is clearly understood. But most business jargon simply complicates your document. Do differentiate between acceptable business vocabulary (such as 'contingency planning' or 'bill of exchange'), for which there is no clear simple alternative, and 'commercialese' (such as 'we beg to acknowledge' or '30th inst.'), which just sounds old-fashioned and pompous. Do not even use acceptable jargon with lay people, unless you are certain they will understand what you mean.

Jargon is very difficult to eradicate; new words and expressions are being added to the business person's vocabulary all the time, and many of them are unnecessary jargon. You need to be on your guard against them because initially they can sound quite impressive—until you realise that they do not actually add anything. So avoid any expressions which do not have a precise meaning which could not be simply expressed in plain English. Here are some examples.

Out of stock situation
We are in receipt of
Assuring you of our best attention

Bottom line (except in the specialised, accountancy, sense)
Advise us (instead of 'tell us')
As per your order
Herewith
Aforesaid
Undermentioned
At your earliest convenience
Please find enclosed
Thanking you in advance
The fact of the matter is
Commence (instead of 'begin')
Forward (instead of 'send')
Flag up
Downside

Two modern forms of jargon which should be avoided are the suffix -wise and the suffix -ise. You will often hear people saying 'That was a good move careerwise', or 'Businesswise, Smith & Co are not doing too well.' Such words have not yet been fully accepted into the English language. At present they are likely to look like bad English to many of your correspondents, and are best avoided.

The suffix -ise is sometimes put at the end of an adjective or noun to turn it into an instant verb. Some such words are now quite acceptable—'standardise', for example. Others are a form of jargon which many people will not understand. They can also often be imprecise. The word 'internationalise' is an example. If you talk about internationalising a manual, what do you mean? Obviously you mean 'to make it international', but how? Is it translated into many languages? Does it use international units? Does it comply with international regulations?

English is an ever-changing language, and today's jargon may become tomorrow's acceptable English. Many words formed with the suffix -ise have already entered the language—'marginalise' is another example. There are therefore no hard and fast rules. The best guide therefore is the one I gave at the beginning of this section. If a word or expression does not have a specific meaning which cannot be simply expressed in plain English, do not use it.

### Avoiding tautology

Tautology means unnecessary repetition—saying the same thing in different words. Some people use it to try to emphasise a point—and fail. There are better ways of emphasising your point. Tautology is poor style; it serves no useful purpose, and simply makes your document long-winded. Here are some examples of tautological expressions commonly used in business communication:

True facts (facts are by their very nature true)
Grateful thanks (thanks are an expression of gratitude)
My personal opinion (how could your opinion be anything but personal?)
Decline to accept ('decline' means 'not accept')
Close proximity (proximity *is* closeness)

There are two other common errors which are not strictly tautology, but which still add unnecessary words to your writing. The first is the expression 'and/or'. This is usually used when the writer means 'and'; it is sometimes used to mean 'or', but there are very few occasions when you actually mean 'and' *and* 'or' at the same time. It is therefore ambiguous as well as long-winded. Just say whichever one you mean.

The second is the practice of putting 'as' before certain words, as in 'as from', 'as and when' and 'as yet'. These expressions mean exactly the same without the 'as'. 'As from' means 'from', 'as and when' means 'when', and 'as yet' means 'yet'.

'As yet' does sometimes serve a purpose. It is often used at the beginning of a sentence to make the meaning clear. For example, you might write:

Yet you have failed to supply our order.

Here 'yet' means 'despite everything'. If you want to say 'until now', you *must* use 'as yet':

As yet you have failed to supply our order.

But this is the only time that 'as yet' should be used.

### Unnecessary abstract nouns

There will obviously be times when you will need to use abstract nouns, but many people seem to be unable to resist using them at every opportunity. As I have said, one of the aims of business communication should be directness, and the concrete is usually more direct than the abstract.

Most abstract nouns make your document sound vague and often pompous. They usually also add to its length. Particularly bad are nouns derived from verbs. There are examples of some of these in the following sentences.

> The reconciliation of your account is in progress. (Your account is being reconciled.)
>
> The achievement of our sales target will not be possible without greater effort on your part. (We need greater effort on your part to achieve our sales target.)
>
> A quick settlement of your account would be appreciated. (Please settle your account quickly).

**Avoiding clichés**

Clichés are words or phrases which have been used so often that they have become old and overworked. They will make your document look artificial and insincere and they are a sign of sloppy writing—they give the impression that you could not be bothered to think of an original expression. Here are some examples:

> Be that as it may
> Needless to say
> I left no stone unturned
> I have explored every avenue
> The fact of the matter is
> Far be it from me
> Last but not least

**Avoiding slang**

Do not let your tone become so conversational that you slip over into slang. The dividing line between the two can be quite fine, so you need to exercise some caution. If you fall on the wrong side of the line, you will give the impression either that you do not know the difference between slang and good English, or that you do not care. Either way, your reader will not be impressed. So avoid slangy expressions like 'OK', 'fed up with', 'on the dot'.

**When to use abbreviations**

Abbreviations give your readers the impression that you cannot be bothered to write the words out in full, and should generally be avoided. The exceptions to this rule are:

- some standard abbreviations which have almost become words in their own right, like Mr, Mrs, Dr, No., plc;

- countries and organisations which are usually referred to by their initials—the USA, the UK, the EU, the CBI, the TUC, the BBC;

- Co. when it is part of a company name, as in John Smith & Co. (but in all other cases, write out 'company')

- the ampersand (&), also when it is part of a company name, as in Jones & Brown plc (but in all other cases, use 'and').

You should avoid using 'etc.' Your correspondence should be specific, and 'etc.' gives the impression that you do not know the full facts or are too lazy to give them. If the list of things you want to mention is too long, use 'for example' or 'such as', rather than 'etc.' So instead of:

> We need to discuss discount, payment terms, minimum order quantities etc.

you should say

> We need to discuss issues such as discount, payment terms and minimum order quantities.

## CHECKLIST

- Do you believe what you are saying, and do you sound as though you do?
- Do you give all the information your reader needs, and is it clear and unambiguous?
- Is your tone conversational without being slangy?
- Is your tone right for the kind of document you are writing and the person you are addressing?
- Do you use the simplest words and expressions you can?
- Does your document contain any jargon, or any terms which might be difficult to understand?
- Are there are unnecessary words or phrases?
- Have you used any clichés?
- If you have used abstract nouns, are they necessary, or could the same idea be expressed more directly?

MEMO

To: Ibrahim Hamed
From: Norman Jameson
Date: 14 May 1995

As you know, I have the deepest respect for you as a manager, and particularly for your sense of fairness. I am sure therefore that you will give the request I am about to make every consideration.

I believe that I have worked hard during the past year, and in particular that I have achieved the goals you kindly set me when I first started in your department. Indeed, you have been good enough to compliment me on my progress on several occasions, for which I am very grateful—it is always helpful to receive encouragement from one's manager, especially when he is as busy as you are.

Being busy, you are probably not aware that it is eighteen months since my salary was last reviewed. Perhaps I should have mentioned it before, but I did not want to bother you and to be honest, I enjoy working in your department so much that I had almost forgotten myself how long it was.

In view of all this, I would be extremely grateful if you could consider raising my salary. I know I can rely on you to decide on a fair figure, given all the circumstances.

Figure 58. A memo making a request in an obsequious way.

To: Ibrahim Hamed
From: Norman Jameson
Date: 14 May 1995

I would like to discuss an increase in my salary commensurate with my progress since joining you department and the level of others on my grade.

As you may know, it is now eighteen months since I started in the department. I enjoy working here very much, and I believe that I have worked hard since I joined, and in particular that I have achieved the goals you set me when I first came here. Indeed, you have commented favourably on my progress on several occasions.

However, in that eighteen months I have not had a salary review, with the result that my pay is beginning to fall behind that of people on a similar grade in other departments.

Figure 59. A memo in which the request is made in the first sentence, thus running the risk of immediate rejection.

# 6
# Techniques for Different Occasions

In Chapter 5 we discussed general points of style which could be applied to most situations. Certain types of correspondence, however, cause particular problems and so warrant special attention. These are:

- requests
- sales letters
- complaints
- accounts queries
- reports

In this chapter, we will look at these categories in more detail, and see what special points of style and technique arise when dealing with them.

## MAKING REQUESTS

In **The right tone for your purpose** in Chapter 5, we saw that the tone of your document will depend partly on whether you are in control or not. If you are making a request, for example, then you are not in control—your success depends very much on how your reader reacts. Your document therefore needs to reflect that. You need to adopt a tone which indicates to your reader that you appreciate that he or she can refuse or agree to your request.

This does not mean that you should be obsequious. The memo shown in figure 58 is *not* a good example of how to get what you want. It is too sycophantic and full of flattery, and sounds false. The reader is more likely to refuse a request expressed in this way. What is needed is a friendly, respectful tone, as in figure 60.

The other point to remember when making a request is to build up to it gradually. Give the background and the reasons for the request first, rather than coming straight out with it. In that way, you prepare your reader's mind, and get him or her thinking more favourably about it. If you ask first and then give your reasons, the reader might subconsciously—or consciously—reject the request before finding out the background. Look at figure 59, and compare it with figure 60. Which request would you be more likely to agree to?

## ANSWERING REQUESTS

When you are *answering* a request, you are in a totally different position—you are in control of the situation. But that does not mean that you can be rude or dismissive. You owe it to your reader to be polite.

The style of your reply to a request will depend on whether you are agreeing to it or refusing it. Each calls for a different approach. The rule of thumb is:

- Say 'yes' quickly, say 'no' slowly.

Let us look at the two styles in more detail.

### Agreeing to a request

There are two rules in agreeing to a request.

1. Do so as **early** in your document as possible.
2. Give the impression that you do so **willingly**.

If you agree with your correspondent's request, then you should say so immediately. Your aim is always to make a good impression on your correspondent, and to do so as soon as possible. Agreeing to the request should make you very popular, so do it at the beginning—preferably in the first paragraph, but certainly no later than the second.

'I think that about covers it...'

MEMO

To: Ibrahim Hamed
From: Norman Jameson
Date: 14 May 1995

As you may know, it is now eighteen months since I started in your department. I enjoy working here very much, and I believe that I have worked well since I joined, and in particular that I have achieved the goals you set me when I first came here. Indeed, you have commented favourably on my progress on several occasions.

However, in that eighteen months I have not had a salary review, with the result that my pay is beginning to fall behind that of people on a similar grade in other departments.

I wonder therefore whether we could discuss an increase in my salary commensurate with my progress in the department and the levels of others on my grade.

Figure 60. A memo building up to a request and couched in a much better tone.

The effect of giving the good news immediately will be wasted, however, if you are grudging or high-handed about it. If you sound as though you are doing your correspondent a great favour, or are acceding to the request grudgingly, you will make quite the wrong impression. Try to sound as though you are pleased to be able to agree.

Figure 61 shows how these guidelines can be put into practice. Jill Lamont tells Patrick Ekwem almost immediately that his request for an increase in discount has been agreed. She does so gracefully, and she makes it sound as though she is pleased to be able to agree. She has to make a proviso, but she leaves that to the end, and takes the sting out of it quite successfully.

### Refusing a request

There are three rules in refusing a request.

1. Do *not* refuse immediately.
2. Be polite.
3. Offer a palliative if possible.

Refusing a request calls for the opposite approach to the one you would adopt if you were agreeing to it. Build up to the refusal gradually. Express an understanding of the writer's problem, explain

**MORGAN & MCCARTHY LTD**
235 Southampton Row
London WC1D 4KJ
Tel 0171-245 7864
Fax 0171-245 0973

21 January 1995

Our Ref. JDL/KM/987432

Mr Patrick Ekwem
Managing Director
Ekwem Enterprises
P O Box 13457
Lagos
Nigeria

Dear Mr Ekwem

I have considered your request, made in your letter of 6 January, for an increase in your discount. Your arguments are extremely persuasive, and I am delighted to be able to agree to your request. All future orders will be supplied at 45 per cent discount.

I hope that this will be the beginning of an even more fruitful relationship between our two companies. As you say, you have steadily increased your turnover with us over the years, and I am sure that the extra discount will give you the incentive to increase it still more.

Of course, you will appreciate that we need a high level of turnover to justify this increased discount, and if your business with us were to fall below its present level, we would have to look at the discount again. However, with the expansion you foresee in the Nigerian market this seems highly unlikely, and I am sure that we shall see your turnover continuing to rise.

Yours sincerely

Jill Lamont
Export Manager

Figure 61. A letter agreeing to a request.

the lengths you have gone to to find a way of solving it, give the reasons for your refusal, and *then* say 'no'. As with agreeing, your aim is to make as good an impression as possible. Building up to your refusal in this way gives you a chance to get your reader at least to understand your position before the disappointment of being turned down.

Once again, this impression can be spoilt if your tone is wrong. Do not think, just because you are in control when refusing a request, that you can be insulting or impolite. Always be courteous when turning someone down. Not only is it good manners, it is in your own interests. If you are refusing a subordinate, it makes sense to try to lessen the disappointment, and not to demotivate him or her. And if it is a member of the public or a client, you have your own or your company's image to consider.

For the same reason, can you somehow soften the blow by offering some hope for the future, no matter how tenuous? You could just say, 'I will get back to you if the situation changes' or 'I will keep your letter on file', or you could offer something specific for the reader to aim for.

Figure 62 shows how Jill Lamont might have written to Patrick Ekwem to refuse his request for an increase in discount. As you can see, she builds up to the refusal gradually; she is polite, even regretful at having to say 'no', and she offers him hope in the form of something to aim at—if he increases his turnover to a certain level, he will be granted the extra discount.

## WRITING SALES LETTERS

Sales letters resemble advertisements, and when writing them, you should be thinking like an advertiser. Adopt an enthusiastic tone and choose positive words; you should pay particular attention to the order in which you present your case.

Enthusiasm is important; if you are not enthusiastic about your product or service, how can you expect your readers to be? So although you should not be so enthusiastic that you mislead your readers, you do need to adopt a positive, up-beat tone.

Similarly, you should use only positive words. If you are talking about a problem the customer might have, to which you have the solution, then you can use words with negative connotations. But otherwise avoid them, and do not use negative words when referring directly to the reader. So you could say:

> Does your office become messy and littered because there is no one with direct responsibility for cleaning it?

But you would put your reader off if you said:

> I will take complete responsibility for your messy and littered office.

In the first sentence, you are only asking if the reader has a messy office. In the second, you are implying that it *is* messy.

**MORGAN & MCCARTHY LTD**
235 Southampton Row
London WC1D 4KJ
Tel 0171-245 7864
Fax 0171-245 0973

21 January 1995

Our Ref. JDL/KM/987432

Mr Patrick Ekwem
Managing Director
Ekwem Enterprises
P O Box 13457
Lagos
Nigeria

Dear Mr Ekwem

Thank you for your letter of 6 January. I take your point about the increase in your turnover with us recently. We are very grateful for your support over the years.

Because of this support, and the good relations between our two companies, I have considered your request carefully, and have looked at it from every angle. I have also consulted my colleagues on the Board of Directors.

Our problem is that there are a number of other customers, in Nigeria and elsewhere, who do more business with us than you do, and who receive the same discount. I am sure you will appreciate that it would not be fair to them if we were to increase your discount without doing the same for them—and increasing everyone's discount would be uneconomic.

I am afraid, therefore, that we cannot agree to your request at present. However, I do not want to be inflexible, and would be very willing to reconsider the position if you were able to increase your turnover a little more. If, therefore, you were to achieve a turnover of £150,000 this year, I would be happy to grant you the discount you ask for. It would then remain at 45 per cent for as long as your turnover was at that level.

Yours sincerely

Jill Lamont
Export Manager

Figure 62. A letter refusing a request.

If you look at the letter in figure 63, you will see that all the words and images associated with Pam Silverman's service are positive—a good corporate image, a pleasing place to work, good staff morale, a complete service. The negative images are all associated with the lack of this service—and none of them is applied directly to the client.

Before you write a sales letter, however, you must be sure that you know who your message is aimed at and what benefits you are offering them.

**Who are you aiming at?**

To be effective, a sales letter should be aimed at a specific market. Many people seem to think that they can write an all-purpose letter which will appeal to a wide range of customers. This is very seldom the case. If you have a product or service that you think will appeal to more than one group of people, then you would be better writing more than one version of your sales letter.

The reason is that you might need to emphasise different aspects of the product or service to appeal to different audiences. The letter in figure 63, for example, is aimed at business people, so Pam writes about a service geared to their needs. A letter to members of the public would obviously have quite a different emphasis.

Not only will the emphasis of your message depend on your audience, so will your language, your tone, and the imagery you use. If you are selling an interior design service to very up-market clients, you will use language that is appropriate. You will talk about decor, style, ambience, quality. On the other hand, if you are writing about the opening of a new bargain store in town, you will talk about special offers, low prices, bargains, free gifts.

So before you start writing, decide exactly who your message is aimed at, and choose an approach and language suited to that market.

**What benefits are you offering?**

Readers of sales letters are not interested in you, nor in your company. They are not even particularly interested in what you are selling. What they want to know about is what you can do for them—what benefits you can offer them.

The benefits might vary according to the audience. Pam Silverman's letter to businesses points out several advantages she can offer; an attractive office environment, a good company image, a service tailored to the company's needs and budget, the only service of its kind in town. If she were writing to personal clients, however, she would offer different benefits: the beauty of flowers as a gift, perhaps,

*Milton Florists*

15 Union Street, Milton, LA24 5JH
Tel. (01231) 987234

30 May 1995

Dear Client

Do you sometimes feel that your offices could do with a little brightening up? Does your reception area look bright and welcoming or drab and discouraging? Do your pot plants tend to wilt and wither because everyone is too busy to care for them properly?

Bright, cheerful premises can make all the difference to an organisation. When clients and visitors come to your office, a colourful floral display in reception will make them feel welcome, and will help your corporate image. And plants and flowers, by making offices attractive places to work in, can improve the morale of staff.

I can help you make your office a happy, welcoming place for staff and visitors alike. My service to businesses—the only one of its kind in Milton—includes:

- a full discussion of your needs
- a survey of the premises to suggest particular plants and flowers for particular locations
- the supply of all plants and flowers
- regular care of plants, from feeding and watering to replacement when necessary
- replacement of all flower arrangements on a regular basis.

Moreover, I can tailor the service to suit your requirements and your budget.

Because I am a fully qualified horticulturist and I always deal with my business clients personally, you can be sure of an expert, professional service. I would be delighted to come and discuss your needs, and to show you how I could help you. Please give me a ring at any time.

Yours sincerely

Pam Silverman

Figure 63. An example of a sales letter.

special rates for weddings and special occasions, a same-day delivery service. It is therefore important to decide on the market you are aiming at, and then to think of all the benefits you can offer that market.

As you think of the benefits, make a list, and then try to put them in order of importance. You need not be too precise—a rough order will do. But get them into order so that when you come to write your letter, you know which are the most important benefits, the ones that need to be emphasised.

### Unique selling propositions and emotional buying triggers

These are two concepts in advertising which can be useful when writing sales letters.

- A **unique selling proposition** (USP) is simply jargon for something which makes your product or service unique, something you have that your competitors do not. In the case of Pam Silverman's florist's shop (figure 63), it is the fact that she will not only supply flowers and plants to businesses, but also ensure that they are cared for and replaced from time to time. It is not essential to have a USP, but if you do have one, then make a point of it in your letter.
- **Emotional buying triggers** are simply appeals to our emotions and instincts. The need to be liked, to project the 'right' image, to achieve, to feel secure, to be an individual—all of these can trigger a buying response if they are given the right stimulus.

### AIDA and the four Ps

When you have decided on your market and the benefits you offer, including any USPs and emotional buying triggers, you need to ensure that you present your letter in a way that is most likely to achieve a sale. There are two ways of presenting a sales letter, called AIDA and the four Ps.

AIDA comes directly from advertising, and is a way of remembering the order in which you should present your case. The letters stand for

Attention
Interest
Desire
Action

In other words, you should first aim to attract your readers' attention.

**C. J. DOBSON PLUMBER**

45 King Street
Brownchurch
Ramshire
Tel. 231906

The Manager
National Midland Bank
5 High Street
Brownchurch

3 September 1994

Dear Sir

Are you trying to bankrupt me? Don't you get enough out of me legally without trying to cheat me as well?

For the last three months, my statements have shown interest charges for an overdraft, together with a 'service charge' of £25 and 'transaction charges' of varying amounts. I was overdrawn by £500 for a short period in May, so I expected to pay a small amount of interest in June, and perhaps a small charge. But I did not expect to be penalised for the next three months. Do you realise that you have taken a total of £150 of my money—and for all I know, my next statement will show a similar amount deducted.

This is not the kind of treatment I expect from my 'friendly High Street bank'. You will please credit my account with the excess you have taken, plus interest, immediately. If I do not receive a corrected statement with a week, I shall take my account elsewhere and report you to the Trading Standards Officer.

Yours faithfully

Charles Dobson

Figure 64. An aggressive letter of complaint.

Then you must hold their interest. Next you need to convert that interest into a desire for your product and or service. And finally you should indicate what action you want them to take.

The four Ps are:

- Promise
- Picture
- Proof
- Push

With this approach, you promise the reader certain benefits. You create a picture showing how he or she will gain those benefits, prove that you can deliver the benefits, and then provide a 'push' to action.

Unlike AIDA, it is not essential to stick to this order, although the 'push' should usually come last.

The two formulae are not mutually exclusive; some of the best sales letters are written so that they conform to both. Figure 63 for example is written according to the AIDA formula. The first paragraph, with its questions, attracts the attention. The next holds the interest, as it shows how flowers and plants can make a difference to an office. The details of the service create a desire for it, and the last sentence prompts the client to action. It also conforms to the four Ps formula. It paints a picture of how Pam's service could change the client's organisation. It promises that the service can be made to benefit the client. It proves that Pam can deliver the benefit by mentioning her qualifications and personal service. And it gives a 'push' towards action.

## MAKING COMPLAINTS

When you are writing to complain about something, do not become aggressive or abusive, especially if it is your first communication. The action—or lack of action—about which you are complaining could well be the result of a genuine error or misunderstanding. We all make mistakes, and it is only common courtesy to give your correspondent the benefit of the doubt.

*Remaining polite and unemotional*

As we saw in Chapter 5, not only is it good manners to be polite and unemotional in your correspondence, but it might be in your own long-term interests. This applies just as much when complaining as in any other business situation. An aggressive approach might get results, but it could be at the expense of your long-term relationship with your correspondent. As always, put yourself in your reader's shoes. How would you react if you received a letter like the one in Figure 64? You would hopefully correct the error, but you would not feel very well disposed towards the writer. If Charles Dobson came to you later for a loan, you might be inclined to be difficult.

Of course, if you have written several times and the error has not been corrected, or if the same error is repeated several times, you will need to be firmer. But you should still be polite. As a rule of thumb, you might adopt a four-stage approach:

1. Write a friendly letter or memo explaining the nature of your complaint and the action you would like taken.

## C. J. DOBSON PLUMBER

45 King Street
Brownchurch
Ramshire
Tel. 231906

Mr Gordon Marshall
Manager
National Midland Bank
Brownchurch

3 September 1994

Dear Mr Marshall

ACCOUNT NO. 43876653

As you know I have been a customer of your bank for many years, and I have always found you and your staff efficient and friendly. I hope therefore that you will be able to correct what I assume is an error in your computer systems.

In May I was overdrawn by £500 for a short period, owing to an unexpected repair on my van. I know that I should have cleared the amount with you, but as I say, the bill was unexpected. I therefore expected to have to pay interest on that amount, as well as a charge for becoming overdrawn without prior clearance. The relevant amounts were shown on my June statement, and I thought that was the end of it.

However, I have had interest, a service charge and transaction charges deducted in July and August as well, with the result that I have paid a total of £150. I am sure that this cannot be correct, and I can only assume that your computer is automatically deducting these charges on the assumption that I am still overdrawn.

I would be grateful, therefore, if you would look into the matter and credit my account with the excess that has been deducted, plus any interest that might have accrued.

I look forward to receiving an amended statement shortly.

Yours sincerely

Charles Dobson

Figure 65. A polite, friendly letter of complaint.

2. If you do not receive a reply, or no action is taken, write again, still in a friendly way, but take a slightly firmer line.

3. If you still do not receive satisfaction, drop the friendly tone, but remain polite.

4. Finally, while remaining polite, threaten some kind of action—withholding payment, reporting your correspondent to the Trading Standards Officer, legal action, whatever is appropriate to the nature of the complaint.

Before you start writing, have two things quite clear in your mind:

- What precisely are you complaining about?
- What do you want done about it?

There is no use in complaining in a general way—about 'poor' service, for example, or 'shoddy' workmanship, or 'late' delivery—unless you have specific details to quote. Your correspondent can only take corrective action if he or she knows *precisely* where things have gone wrong.

Similarly, your correspondent can do little more than apologise if you do not say what corrective action you want taken. This action may simply be to improve the service, workmanship or delivery you receive, but even then, you should try to be specific. What level of service do you expect? What do you regard as a satisfactory delivery time? And of course, many complaints require more specific action—to issue a credit note, to replace faulty goods or to compensate you for financial loss.

With the answers to these questions, you will be able to write your letter or memo, which should be in three parts:

1. A polite introduction, perhaps pointing out the good relationship you have enjoyed with your correspondent so far.

2. The specific details of your complaint.

3. A request for corrective action.

Figure 65 shows a letter based on this format. It is friendly and clear, and it should achieve Charles Dobson's objective just as well as the letter in figure 64, while keeping his relationship with his bank manager on a friendly basis.

**CARLTON & DAVIES**

*BUILDING CONTRACTORS*

24 Queen Street, Morganston, Lancashire, MG2 7UH

Our Ref. MD/KR/19876

Mr J. P. Singh
5 Brooms Close
Morganston
MG4 9KN

8 February 1995

Dear Mr Singh

I was very concerned to see from your letter of 31 January that you were not satisfied with our response to your request for repairs to be made to your roof.

On receipt of your letter, I conducted a thorough investigation of all the circumstances of the job. I spoke to our telephonist, our Works Manager and the men who carried out the work.

What happened, as I understand it, is that you telephoned us on 15 January to say that there was a leak in your roof, and that the rain was coming in. Because of the storms, we had a great many emergency calls that day, and you were told by the telephonist that someone would call as soon as possible. She also, I believe, advised you on short-term measures you could take to alleviate the problem. You confirmed that you would be at home for the rest of the day.

Our workmen did in fact call later—at about eight o'clock, according to their worksheet—but you were not at home. You say that they should have made the necessary repairs in your absence but unfortunately, in order to do so, they needed access to the house. I believe that they left a note to that effect. They did, however, call again next day, when you were in. As you say, the repair they made then was only temporary, but the men concerned tell me that they did point that out to you at the time. I am very sorry if you misunderstood them. The reason for the temporary repair was that we were still receiving emergency calls. To make a permanent repair would have taken several hours, and they were certain that their temporary job would hold until they were able to return and finish it—as in fact it did.

They returned a week later to complete the job. You say that you should not have had to wait that long, but as I have said, we had a great many emergencies to deal with. It was therefore not possible to come back any sooner, and the temporary repair did ensure that in the meantime you did not suffer any inconvenience.

I agree that our service was not as fast as we would normally like it to be, but I am sure you will appreciate that the situation was not normal. I do believe that under the circumstances we did everything possible to accommodate you. I am afraid therefore that we cannot agree to waive our charge for the repair.

Yours sincerely

Martin Davies
Director

Figure 66. A letter rejecting a customer's complaint.

## ANSWERING COMPLAINTS

How can we turn a complaining customer into a satisfied one? It is not too difficult. All it needs is a friendly approach, a conciliatory attitude and a willingness to take any action necessary if you are at fault. Even if you are rejecting the complaint, it is possible to do so without causing offence.

The answer to a complaint can be divided into two or three parts, depending on whether you are accepting or rejecting it.

- the apology
- the explanation
- the remedy if you accept the complaint

### The apology

Notice that I did not say 'if you accept the complaint' after 'the apology' above. That is because the way to keep your correspondent happy is to 'apologise' whatever the outcome. So even if you are rejecting the complaint, try to find something to apologise for, or to express concern about. Here are a few examples of things you can say:

- I was very concerned to hear that you are dissatisfied with our service.
- I am very sorry if our terms of trade were not clear, but if you look closely at item 12...
- I am sorry if I did not make myself clear in my last letter.
- I am sorry if you misunderstood the terms of our agreement.

Nobody likes to be told that they are wrong, even if they know that they are—least of all customers. They might misunderstand or misinterpret things, but they are not wrong. But do not take the apology too far. You can apologise for not making yourself clear, but do not actually say that you are wrong just to be nice to your correspondent. That could set an awkward precedent and cause a great many problems.

If you apologise for a late delivery, for example, when it was the customer's fault that the delivery was late, then you could lay yourself open to a claim for compensation. Taking another example, if you agree that your service was poor, then the customer will expect an improvement. If in fact you did everything possible to help him or her, you will not be able to make any improvements and the customer is likely to be disappointed again. Explain the situation fully, apologise for any misunderstanding and be friendly, but state clearly that you believe you are right.

If you *are* wrong, of course, you should admit it and apologise. You can even make your correspondent feel that he or she has done you a favour by expressing your thanks. Here are some examples:

- We always welcome our customers' views on our service, as it is only through this feedback that we can improve. I am only sorry that we have treated you so badly.
- Thank you for raising the matter with me. Your letter has highlighted a fault in our system which we are now able to correct. I do apologise, however, for the inconvenience you have been caused.

Note how, in the last example, the writer apologises for '*the* inconvenience you have been caused', not '*any* inconvenience caused', which is a phrase so often used. There is no question about whether the customer has been caused any inconvenience or not. The very fact the he or she has had to write to you is in itself an inconvenience. If you have to apologise, do so unreservedly. Too often, people in business seem to try to hide behind bland, formal phrases and sentences when apologising, as if trying to avoid responsibility. 'We regret any inconvenience caused' is just such a sentence. It seems to imply:

(a) that the writer does not believe that you have really been inconvenienced;

(b) that if you have, it is not really anyone's fault, and is a cause for regret rather than apology; and

(c) that if it is anyone's responsibility it is the company's ('we') rather than the individuals ('I').

The other way in which some people try to avoid responsibility is by making excuses. They give details of how their supplier has let them down, or explain at great length how short-staffed they are, or blame the whole thing on someone who has now left the company, and in the process they seem to forget to apologise.

Why do business people still write like this? Most of us would feel much better disposed towards someone who accepted responsibility, apologised and took corrective action than towards someone who tried to make excuses and corrected the error grudgingly and without apology. By all means explain the circumstances behind the error (see below), but do so briefly, and do not think that your explanation is a substitute for an apology.

### The explanation

When you have apologised, you should give some explanation of the facts of the case. The way in which you explain will depend on whether you are accepting or rejecting the complaint.

If you agree that your correspondent has genuine cause for complaint, then it is a good idea to give some explanation of what went wrong. But do not let your explanation get in the way of your apology. The apology comes first so that the explanation does not look like an excuse.

You should also not go into too much detail. By all means say that you were let down by your suppliers, or that you were short-staffed at the time, or that your system for dealing with orders was at fault, but then leave it at that. Complainants, sadly, are not usually interested in your problems. What they want is an apology and a remedy. The explanation might make them more understanding, but only if you keep it brief.

If you are rejecting the complaint, your explanation needs to be rather longer. There are three rules for this kind of explanation.

1. Always give the impression that you have investigated the complaint fully, no matter how trivial it really is. (But avoid the mistake that a railway executive was once said to have made. A passenger wrote complaining that he had been bitten by a flea while travelling to Scotland. The executive replied at length, explaining how thoroughly he had investigated the complaint, but his secretary inadvertently enclosed the passenger's original letter with his reply. Across the bottom was written 'Miss Smith—please send standard "flea" letter.')

2. Give all the facts as you understand them, particularly where your understanding differs from that of your correspondent.

3. If there are other people who can back up your version of events, then say who they are.

Figure 66 is an example of a letter rejecting a complaint, which shows how these rules can be applied. It also shows some of the techniques explained under **The apology** above.

### The remedy

In the final part of your letter (before you sign off, perhaps with another brief apology) outline how you intend to remedy the situation.

**NEW MODE FASHIONS**
5 Thornton Road, Langton, SR15 4RT
(01234) 98765

Our Ref. GH/SW

12 July 1995

Mrs J. Wilson
Hilton & Co
46 Kilsey Street
Osberton
OS1 2TG

Dear Mrs Wilson

I was extremely sorry to see from your letter of 5 July that your special order of 20 June was delivered late. I am grateful to you, however, for giving me such full details of the order and delivery, as it has enabled me to trace and correct a fault in our order processing system.

What apparently happened was that the order was held back because the computer showed a query on your account. By the time we discovered that the query was due to a computer error, the consignment was late. We have now corrected the computer error and instituted a system for informing customers immediately if there is likely to be any delay in the despatch of their orders.

This means that this problem should not arise again, but I realise that that does not solve your immediate problem, which is that your customer has cancelled her order. I would therefore like to make the following two suggestions.

1. We will cancel our invoice for the garments, enabling you to give them to your customer free of charge as a means of regaining her goodwill.
2. We will in addition credit you with the full value of the order, to compensate you for the loss of business you have suffered.

I hope that these suggestions meet with your approval, and that you will accept my apologies for the inconvenience you have been caused.

Yours sincerely

Gillian Holding
Managing Director

Figure 67. A letter agreeing with a customer's complaint and offering a remedy.

This could simply involve changes to your systems or your way of doing things so that the same mistake does not happen again. Or it could take a more concrete form, such as giving the complainant a credit note, cancelling an invoice or paying some form of compensation. It all depends on the circumstances.

But do remember that goodwill is important in any business relationship. If you have committed an error or inconvenienced a business contact in any way, it is worth a bit of trouble, and even money, to ensure that the goodwill is not lost. So when it comes to a remedy, err on the side of generosity.

Figure 67 shows a letter accepting a complaint. It includes all the elements we have talked about, from a graceful and unreserved apology to a brief explanation of what went wrong and then to a generous suggestion for remedying the situation.

## ACCOUNTS QUERIES

One of the hardest letters to get right is the one designed to sort out a situation where two organisations' accounts have become bogged down in a mass of invoices, counter-invoices and credit notes to the extent that they cannot agree on what is owed. In this kind of situation, every letter seems to add yet further complexity; it requires a lot of research, a lot of patience, clear thinking and clear writing to unravel it all. Clear writing is particularly important in this kind of letter. Do make quite sure that there is no ambiguity or vagueness in your letter, because there must be absolutely no further misunderstanding to muddy the waters.

There are four stages to this task.

1. Assemble *all* the information which is remotely relevant to the account. This means every invoice, every credit note, every statement, every letter received or written, by you or anyone else, any notes (or memories) of telephone conversations.

2. Go through it all, preferably in chronological order. Make sure that you have a copy of every document referred to in the correspondence and every invoice and credit note referred to in the statement. If there are any items you do not have, and they cannot be found, make a note. Read everything, several times if necessary, until you fully understand what has happened. It can sometimes help to make notes as you go along, but however you do it, make sure that it is all quite clear in your mind.

**FRANCIS MONK & CO LTD**
6 High Street
Midchester
MC1 4GF
(01324) 123456

Wendy Cartwright
Financial Director
Canter Distribution Ltd
5 Jarvis Way
Branston
BT3 7YH

9 March 1995

Dear Ms Cartwright

Thank you for your letter of 2 March, sent with your February statement. Perhaps if I explain, item by item, what our understanding is of the situation between our two companies, we can resolve this dispute once and for all.

Invoice 14235. This was paid on 25 October with our cheque No. 015943, which was cleared on 10 November. My colleague Henry Thompson asked for this item to be cleared from our statement in his letter of 6 January, but it has not yet been done.

Invoice 14425. This invoice was charged at the wrong discount. On 22 January Henry Thompson wrote and asked for a credit note to amend the discount. Your colleague Lawrence Davies wrote to him on 5 February to say that instead of issuing a credit note, you would cancel this invoice and issue a new one.

Invoice 14457. This is for exactly the same goods as invoice 14425. Since we did not order two consignments, I assume that it was intended to cancel invoice 14425, although nothing to that effect appears on the invoice itself. On 3 February, I wrote asking whether this was the case. The only reply I received was an unsigned letter dated 10 February saying that the invoice was correct, but with no further explanation.

Invoice 14534. I agree this invoice.

Credit Note 10987. This relates to faulty goods received on invoice 14534, and is correct.

Invoice 14768. I agree this invoice.

Invoice 14784. I agree this invoice.

Credit Note 11259. There is no mention on this credit note of what it relates to. From the amount, I assume that it is to correct invoice 14425, on which we were given the wrong discount (see above).

Missing from your statement is any reference to *our* invoice 08976 of 6 February (copy attached), relating to the return of goods. I can confirm that the goods were delivered—our delivery note is signed by Ted Victor.

The correct position, as I see it, is therefore as follows:

| | |
|---|---|
| Amount due, as per statement: | £1,862.79 |
| Less invoice 14235, already paid: | (£234.63) |
| Less invoice 14425, which should have been cancelled: | (£526.46) |
| Add credit note 11259, which should not have been raised: | £96.23 |
| Less our invoice 08976: | (£186.54) |
| Actual amount due: | £1,011.39 |

If you agree with my analysis, I would be grateful if you could send me an amended statement. As soon as I receive it, I shall send you a cheque for the full amount. If you do not agree with my understanding of the position, perhaps you could let me know what in particular you disagree with, and let me have details of how your view differs from mine.

Yours sincerely

Brian Wagstaff
Chief Accountant

Figure 68. A letter clarifying a complicated accounts query.

3. Write your letter, setting out the situation as you now understand it, in a clear and logical sequence. Depending on circumstances, the clearest sequence might be chronological order, numerical order by invoice, or the order in which the items appear on the statement. But do make sure that you have chosen the best order in which to present the facts. Explain how each document mentioned fits (or does not fit) into the picture and give a summary of the situation (who owes what). If your correspondent refers to documents which you do not have, ask for copies. If you mention documents (particularly invoices and credit notes) which he or she does not appear to have, then enclose copies.
4. Do not give your correspondent a chance to introduce any confusion into the situation. Insist that:
   (a) if they agree with your analysis, they should pay the amount owed or amend their statement; or
   (b) if they disagree, they should indicate what particular item or items they disagree with and provide documentation to support their case.

In other words, ensure that any further correspondence relates to your analysis. You then have a better chance of resolving the confusion.

If you follow these four stages, your letter should have the desired result. But the most important steps are probably the first two. If you do not have all the information in front of you, and if you do not fully understand the situation yourself, then your letter will probably just cloud the issue still further.

Figure 68 shows how a letter of this kind should look. It is clear, each document is presented and explained, there is a summary of what Brian Wagstaff believes his company owes, and there is a clear statement of what he expects Wendy Cartwright to do next.

## REPORTS

A good report is a joy to read—clear, concise, well argued and to the point. It leaves no signs of the effort that has gone into making it like that! Good reports take time and care, and have their own techniques.

### Assembling the facts

Whatever kind of report you are writing, you will be gathering facts. Facts are the basis of any report, and before you even begin to plan your report, you should make sure that you have all the relevant facts.

And this means *all* the facts. Do not just gather those facts which fit some preconceived idea you may have and ignore everything else. That is dishonest, it invalidates the whole report (which is of no use if it is not objective), and there is a strong chance that someone reading it will know some of the facts that you have left out.

And do not just select information which seems to be especially relevant and ignore anything which looks less important. Until you start to sift and analyse your facts, you will not know how important each piece of information is.

The trick in writing reports is to make them as short as you can while still including everything that is relevant. This requires sifting and selection of what to include and what to leave out. But this process should take place *after* you have assembled all your information, not while you are doing it.

Your style can also help you here. You can include more information in less space if you use clear, concise language and a brief style. But beware. Your report should also be easy to read; if you are too terse, people will find it difficult. It is a question of balance. If you look at the extracts from reports shown in this book, you will see how they combine conciseness with an easy flow.

## Seeing both sides

If you are presenting a report on a subject capable of more than one interpretation, or on which people can hold more than one opinion, you need to present both sides of the argument, and this means that you must be able to *see* both sides yourself. An objective report weighs up the various arguments and then makes recommendations or reaches conclusions based on the most convincing one. Show your readers that you have considered all the facts, that you have looked at the situation from all sides and that your conclusions are based on an objective assessment. If you do not, it will soon become apparent, and your report will lose its credibility.

Just as some people think that they can influence their readers by only including facts which support their point of view, so there are some who believe that they can do the same thing by ignoring any interpretation of the facts except their own. Do not be tempted to try it. You may get away with it, but the chances are that you will not. At least one of your readers may realise that other interpretations are possible: you could then find yourself faced with awkward questions for which you are not prepared.

### Presenting your case

When you have considered all the facts objectively, and reached your conclusion, that is the time to be persuasive. Argue logically as we discussed in Chapter 2. Introduce facts from your analysis to back up your arguments and present your own or other people's opinions if necessary. No one is going to object if you favour one solution or one side of the argument at this stage—they will expect you to. But do show that you have considered the facts objectively.

If you are presenting opinions, however, ensure that your readers are well aware that they *are* opinions. Do not mix facts with opinions. If you present something as a fact, then make sure that you have the information to back it up. If it is an opinion, then say something like:

This is believed to be the case...
My opinion is...
In my opinion...
I believe that...

Figure 69 overleaf shows the 'Conclusion' section of a report; in it the writer argues persuasively and logically, and is quite clear about what is fact and what is opinion.

### Dealing with opposing arguments

When you are discussing something at a meeting, other people can question you and argue against you, and you in turn can refute their arguments. When writing a report, you still need to deal with those arguments and questions as far as possible, but you do not have the opportunity to hear what they are. You therefore need to anticipate them and answer them in the course of the report.

If you have considered all sides of the argument when assessing your information, then you should not find it too hard to anticipate what the opposing arguments might be—you will probably have thought of most of them while doing your assessment. Since you will have considered these points before coming to your conclusion, you will also know what arguments you used when rejecting them.

But it is as well to think long and hard about this, and to make sure that there are no contrary arguments that you have not considered. The aim is to persuade your readers to accept your recommendation, without having the issue clouded by an argument you could have refuted if only you had thought of it. Figure 69 shows how to anticipate and deal with such arguments. Notice that the writer does not specifically say, 'It could be argued that... but my counter-

CONCLUSION

The above analysis leads me to the conclusion that handling our own sales and distribution is a perfectly feasible option. We have the space to do all our own storage. Of course the space we have is not a warehouse as such, but do we actually need a warehouse? The outhouse is dry, secure and spacious, and could very easily and cheaply be adapted to our needs. As I have said, all that is necessary is shelving.

Our computer is quite capable of handling all our invoicing, and although we do not currently have the necessary software, that is something that can readily be purchased. The approximate cost of such a package is given in Appendix B, but since at this stage we are concerned only with the feasibility of the project, not its precise cost, I have not investigated the costs and advantages of the various packages.

We would obviously have to take on extra staff, and it has been said that this in itself would make the project unviable. However, it need not be so. I estimate that we would only need the equivalent of two extra in-house staff to handle the order processing, packing and invoicing. We could certainly afford this kind of increase in our staffing level. As for sales representatives, we need not employ our own. If we used freelance representatives, we would pay them on a commission only basis, as suggested in Section 3. Although some people do not like employing freelance representatives on the grounds that they would not be fully committed to our products, my opinion is that they are likely to more committed to us than our present distributors are. We would be a big fish in their little ponds, whereas to our present distributors, we are very small fry indeed.

In the light of all this, I believe that handling our own distribution is not only feasible, it is also desirable.

Figure 69. The 'Conclusion' section of a report, arguing the writer's case and refuting contrary arguments.

argument is...' The techniques used are:

- The space we have...but
- Although we do not currently have the necessary software...
- It has been said....but...
- Although some people do not like...

## CHECKLIST

- When making a request, is your language polite without being obsequious?
- Do you build up to the request, giving the background and the reasons first?
- If you are agreeing to a request, do you agree within the first two paragraphs of your communication?
- If you are rejecting a request, do you build up to the rejection gradually, and do you try to soften the blow?
- In sales letters, do you know who your message is aimed at?
- Do you know what benefits you are offering?
- Does your sales letter follow the AIDA or four Ps formula?
- Is your tone enthusiastic and your language positive?
- If you are making a complaint, is it clear precisely what you are complaining about?
- Do you say what you want done about it?
- If you are answering a justified complaint, do you apologise unreservedly?
- If you are rejecting a complaint, can you nevertheless find something to apologise for?
- Have you said that you are wrong when you do not believe you are?
- Do you give an explanation of the position?
- If you are at fault, do you offer a remedy?
- If you are dealing with a complicated accounts query, do you have all the information, and do you understand it all?
- Is your document clearly and logically presented?
- Do you give your correspondent any opportunity to introduce further complications?
- If you are writing a report, have you assembled all the facts?
- Do you present both sides of any potentially controversial subject?
- Do you present your case logically, and back up your statements with facts?
- Do you deal with opposing arguments?

# 7
# Improving Your Grammar

If words are the building blocks of your document, which you use to build sentences and paragraphs, then grammar is the mortar that holds them together. If you do not know how to use the words you choose, and the rules for putting them together, then your correspondence will consist of a jumble of unconnected words and phrases.

Some people cannot see the need for good grammar; they argue that as long as your readers can understand what you are saying, it does not have to be grammatically correct. There are two problems with this argument. The first is that a document full of badly constructed sentences reflects badly on you. It is clumsy to read and it looks sloppy. The second is that a badly constructed sentence may be understandable in one context, but the same poor construction in another sentence could make it vague or misleading. Look at these two sentences:

> We have a model with a 1.5 litre engine which has aluminium wheels.

> We have a model with a 1.5 litre engine which is guaranteed against corrosion.

Both sentences are incorrect, because the qualifying clauses 'which has aluminium wheels' and 'which is guaranteed...' are not close enough to the noun they qualify, 'model'. However, with the first one, the reader at least knows what is meant, simply because an engine does not have wheels. The second one, which contains the same error, could be read in two ways—either the model is guaranteed against corrosion or the engine is. But which? So someone who is not concerned about grammar is likely to write a document that not only looks clumsy, but is difficult to understand.

In order to write well you do not need to have a detailed knowledge of grammar, but you should know some of the basic rules. This chapter will therefore not deal with the theoretical detail. What it will do is explain some of the basics of grammar and illustrate some of the errors most often found in business writing. It will also explain where you can occasionally break the rules to create a better flow or effect. But remember, there is a world of difference between knowing the rules and breaking them for effect and not knowing them and breaking them through ignorance.

Words are divided into different types, each with a particular role to play in building up a sentence. These divisions are known as **parts of speech**, and here we will look at each in turn.

## NOUNS AND PRONOUNS

Nouns and pronouns are 'naming' words. They identify what it is we are talking about—for example, contract, client, him, she, Jennifer. As we saw in Chapter 4 every sentence must have a **subject**, and the subject will always be either a **noun** or a **pronoun**.

Every sentence must also have a **predicate**, and the predicate can either be just a **verb** ('He retired'), or a verb and an **object**. So if the verb tells us what the subject did, the object tells us what the subject did it to.

The object will also always be a noun or a pronoun. So in the sentence 'We have stopped the account', 'we' is the subject, 'have stopped' is the verb (that is what we did) and 'the account' is the object (that is what we did it to).

### Using nouns

Nouns are the words which actually name objects, places, people, ideas, etc. There are five kinds:

- **common nouns**, which name objects, like letter, desk, man;
- **abstract nouns**, which name things you cannot see or touch, like strategy, export, idea;

- **proper nouns**, which name specific people or places, like Peter, London, the Prime Minister;
- **collective nouns**, which name collections of people or things, like board, committee;
- **compound nouns**, which consist of more than one word, like Peter Smith, John Brown & Co, Peters & Jones.

## Nouns—potential problems

By and large, we do not need to worry too much about the differences between different kinds of noun, but there are one or two grammatical rules which concern specific types, and which sometimes cause problems.

*1. Proper nouns*

A proper noun, but only a proper noun, should start with a capital letter. In other words, when you are writing the name or title of a person, an organisation, a country or an institution, use a capital letter—Peter Smith, London, Thailand, Hampshire County Council, the Managing Director, but not the Balance Sheet, the Product, the Sales Figures. Some words can be either proper or common nouns, depending on the context. You might, for instance, write about the Government, but about a government. In the first instance, you are talking about a particular government, so the word is a title—a proper noun. In the second, you are talking about any government, so it is a common noun.

*2. Collective and compound nouns*

These are singular—they are one entity—even though they consist of several individuals. A committee of ten people is singular, because it is only one committee. Jones & Peterson is singular because, although Jones and Peterson are two people, they form just one company. They must therefore take singular verbs. So you would write: 'The Board has decided to appoint a new director', not 'The Board *have* decided...' 'Jones & Peterson owes us money' not 'Jones & Peterson *owe* us money.' The only exception to this rule is when you are talking about a committee, board etc. as individual people; then you should use a plural verb. So you would write 'The Board went their separate ways.'

Two common nouns connected by 'and' will normally be regarded as two nouns and therefore take a plural verb. But there are one or two expressions made up in this way which express one idea or concept, and which are therefore compound nouns. An example is 'bread and butter', as in 'The company's bread and butter is its retail trade'. In this context, 'bread and butter' is a single concept, not actual bread and butter, and so it takes a singular verb.

*3. Verbal nouns*

You will find yourself using participles (see under **verbs** below) as **verbal nouns** (called **gerunds**). You should learn to recognise them for what they are and treat them as nouns. They are normally the present participles, ending in -ing, as in 'asking', 'looking', 'writing'. This form of the verb has other uses, however, so you will have to recognise when it is being used as a noun. Look at the following sentences:

> I look forward to him coming to visit us.
> I could see him coming a mile away.

One of these sentences is wrong. Can you see which one?

The first sentence contains a very common mistake. The object of the sentence is 'coming', which is used as a gerund. So, like any noun, it must take the possessive form of the pronoun, 'his'. 'I look forward to his coming...' If the object were another noun, say 'report', you would not say 'I look forward to him report', so you cannot say 'him coming'.

The test is to say 'what?' after the verb, and see what answer you get. So in the first sentence, you would say 'I look forward to what?' The answer is 'coming', which is therefore a noun. In the second sentence, you would say 'I could see what?' The answer is 'him'. 'Coming' is therefore not a noun—it describes 'him'.

## Using pronouns

Pronouns are words which take the place of nouns. They are extremely valuable little words; without them, documents would be clumsy and difficult to read. Consider the following passage:

> Jennifer Jameson has the draft contract. Peter Denton will ask Jennifer Jameson to give the draft contract to Sarah Miller so that Sarah Miller can check the draft contract to make sure that Jennifer Jameson has not overlooked any errors in the draft contract.

That is a very long-winded and difficult passage. How much simpler it is when you use pronouns:

> Jennifer Jameson has the draft contract. **I** will ask **her** to give it to **you** so that **you** can make sure that **she** has not overlooked any errors in **it**.

There are seven kinds of pronoun:

- **personal pronouns**, which relate to particular people or things, like I, you, her, it;
- **possessive pronouns**, which, as their name implies, indicate possession, like his, her, my, our, your;
- **reflexive pronouns**, which are used when the object of a verb is the same as the subject: himself, myself, themselves, as in 'He hurt himself';
- **demonstrative pronouns**, which point something out, like this, that, those;
- **relative pronouns**, which introduce clauses which qualify a preceding noun or pronoun like 'which' in the above passage;
- **interrogative pronouns**, which ask questions, like who?, what?, which?;
- **indefinite pronouns**, like anybody, something.

### Pronouns—potential problems

As with nouns, you do not need to identify each category of pronoun, but there are certain common errors with particular types, which you should watch out for.

*1. Ambiguous use*

Ensure that your use of pronouns is not ambiguous. If it is, then either use the appropriate nouns instead or find another way of expressing yourself. A common ambiguity is this kind of thing: 'John Smith talked to Peter Brown about his letter.' Whose letter is it—John Smith's or Peter Brown's?

*2. A relative pronoun cannot start a sentence*

Because it takes the place of a noun, a pronoun can usually be the subject of a sentence, and can therefore start the sentence. The only exception is the **relative pronoun**. Because relative pronouns introduce *clauses*, not sentences (see under **Phrases and clauses** below), you cannot start a sentence with one. It is wrong therefore to say:

> Thank you for your order. Which is being processed today.

'Which' should introduce a clause, which is part of a sentence. So the passage should read:

> Thank you for your order, which is being processed today.

*A relative pronoun must relate back*

A relative pronoun must also relate back to a noun or pronoun earlier in the sentence. You cannot therefore say:

> Our delivery was late, which meant that we could not supply your order on time.

The only noun in the first part of that sentence is 'delivery', and 'which' does not refer to it. So the relative pronoun is left hanging in the air. You should therefore say:

> Our delivery was late so we could not supply... *or*
>
> Our delivery was late, and we could therefore not supply...

*4. Personal pronouns: subjective and objective*

Some people seem to have problems with the different forms of the personal pronoun. There are two forms—the **subjective** and the **objective**. I, he, she, they are subjective. As their name implies, they are used when they are the subject of the sentence. Me, him, her, them are objective, and are used when they are the object of the sentence.

However, many people have difficulty deciding which form to use, particularly when the pronoun is used in combination. For example, can you see what is wrong with the following sentences?

> Our Sales Manager and me will call on you tomorrow.
> The Board would like to see you and I at ten o'clock tomorrow.

They both use the wrong form of the pronoun. The best way to ensure that you use the right form is to use the pronoun on its own. So in the first sentence, you would drop 'Our Sales Manager'. What would you say if it were just you calling on the client? You would say 'I will call...' So you should say 'Our Sales Manager and I...' Similarly in the second sentence, if it were just you that the Board wanted to see, you would say, 'The Board would like to see me...' So you should say 'you and me...'

*The pronoun 'none'*

A pronoun which causes some difficulty is the word 'none'. Can you see what is wrong with the following sentence?

> None of the committee's suggestions are acceptable to the Board.

'None' is short for 'not one', and is therefore singular. So it should always take a singular verb. The above sentence should read 'None of the committee's suggestions *is* acceptable.'

## VERBS

### Explanation

Verbs are 'doing' or 'being' words. They tell us what the subject of a sentence does or did, is or was. As we saw in Chapter 4, every sentence must have a verb. There are many different forms of verbs, and we do not need to understand them all. In order to understand some of the problems you might encounter, however, you need to know that:

- the **infinitive** is the 'to' form of the verb—'to write', 'to meet', 'to complain';
- verbs have two **voices**—active and passive. In the **active voice**, the subject of the verb is doing the action, as in 'The firm *reassured* the client'. In the **passive voice**, the subject is having the action done to him, her or it, as in 'The client *was reassured* by your letter.'
- many forms of the verb are **compounds**. They are made up of the verbs 'to have' and 'to be' (known as **auxiliary** verbs) with a form of the verb itself tagged on. The form of the verb itself which is tagged on is called a **participle**. 'Written', for example, is the **past participle**, and 'writing' is the **present participle**.

### Potential problems

Some of the problems you might encounter with verbs are as follows:

*1. Too much use of the passive voice*

This makes a communication seem impersonal. It can also make it look weak. Compare the following two versions of the same sentence:

> Your account has been credited.
> I have credited your account.

The second version, which is in the active voice (the subject is performing the action), is very much more positive, direct and personal. The general rule therefore is to prefer the active voice. But it is a stylistic rather than a grammatical rule, and you do not need to follow it rigidly. If there is a particularly important noun, you might want to make it the subject of the sentence, thus giving it more emphasis. In a sales letter, for example, it might be better to say 'Our service has been recommended by all the leading hotels in the area', thus emphasising 'our service', rather than 'All the leading hotels in the area recommend our service.'

*2. Split infinitives*

The rules of grammar say that you should not split your infinitive. This means that nothing should come between 'to' and the rest of the verb. Do not for example say 'I would like to sincerely apologise for our error'. In trying to avoid splitting the infinitive, there are three places you can put the word which is splitting it: before the infinitive, after the infinitive, or at the end of the sentence. When you are faced with a split infinitive, try all three to see which sounds better. In the above example, your choices would be:

> I would like sincerely **to apologise** for our error.
> I would like **to apologise** sincerely for our error.
> I would like **to apologise** for our error sincerely.

In this case, the second version sounds better, but there will be other sentences in which one of the other positions would be better.

However, you do not need to be too dogmatic. In most cases, you should be able to avoid splitting your infinitives, and you will find that your sentences read more smoothly as a result. But there will be times, particularly in longer sentences, when it will actually sound *less* clumsy with the infinitive split. Take a sentence like this:

> We appear to deliberately avoid making our clients feel at home while they are waiting to see a partner.

Try the three 'non-split' versions. Although putting 'deliberately' before the infinitive is the best of the three, the sentence probably reads better with the infinitive split.

*4. Verb and subject must agree in number*

The verb and the subject in a sentence must agree in number. If the subject is plural then the verb must also be plural. If the subject is singular then the verb too must be singular. We discussed some aspects of this when dealing with collective and compound nouns above, but it can also present problems in other ways.

Generally, two nouns joined by 'and' form a plural subject—there are two people or things. However, the adjectives 'each' and 'every' have the effect of making nouns singular. So you would say:

> Every director and manager *is* entitled to a company car.

If you are talking about each or every director and manager, you are talking about them individually, so they are singular.

You should also beware of phrases or clauses which are in parenthesis (written almost as an aside). You would write:

> The desk and the typewriter are to be moved to the new office.

There are two things to be moved so the subject is plural. But you would write:

> The desk, together with the typewriter, *is* to be moved to the new office.

In this sentence, the typewriter is mentioned as an aside, almost as an afterthought. The subject is actually just the desk, so the verb is singular.

The other common problem with getting the subject and the verb to agree, is that if they become separated, it can be difficult to see what the subject actually is. Can you see what is wrong with these two sentences?

> The aim of these proposals are to make the company more productive.

> My expenses, including subsistence allowance, is attached.

In the first sentence, the subject is 'aim', not 'proposals', so the verb should be singular. In the second, the subject is 'expenses', not 'allowance', so the verb should be plural.

A useful test to check what the subject is, is simply to say 'what?' before the predicate. So in the first sentence, you would ask 'What is to make the company more productive?' The answer is 'the aim'. In the second sentence, you would ask 'What are attached?' The answer is 'my expenses'.

## ADJECTIVES AND ADVERBS

Adjectives and adverbs are 'qualifying' words. They add to and extend the meaning of other words. As we saw in Chapter 5, one of the main stylistic errors people make is to use vague or meaningless qualifiers—nice, significant, quite. Used correctly, adjectives and adverbs can help you express yourself more precisely and add considerably to your readers' understanding of your document. Used badly, they will just lengthen it and make it hard to understand.

### Using adjectives

Adjectives qualify (describe) nouns. 'A productive meeting', 'the correct spelling', 'an easy decision'—these are all examples of adjectives in action. Participles (see under **Verbs** above) can be used as adjectives, as in 'a written contract' (past participle) or 'a leaking tap' (present participle).

Adjectives can describe things or they can compare them, as in 'the best car on the market' or 'This car is better than that one'. The -er form is called the **comparative**, and is used for comparing two things. The -est form is the **superlative**, and is used when there are three or more.

The words 'the', 'a' and 'an' qualify nouns, so they are adjectives, although they are usually called articles. 'The' is the definite article (it means you are talking about something specific and definite) and 'a' and 'an' are indefinite articles (they mean you are talking about something indefinite).

## Adjectives – potential problems

*1. Comparatives*

The comparative form of the adjective is used to compare two things. This is an easy rule to follow when you are making a direct comparison, as in 'Norma's idea is better than Ken's.' It sounds quite wrong to say 'Norma's idea is best than Ken's', and few people would make that mistake. But what about the following?

Of the two plans Norma's is the best.

That does not sound quite so wrong, but you are still comparing two things, so you should in fact be using the comparative form. It should be:

Of the two plans Norma's is better.

Even with this construction, you should use the comparative when comparing two things and the superlative only when comparing three or more.

*2. Articles*

When you are writing about two people or things, you can sometimes leave out the definite or indefinite article, but in other contexts the omission can cause confusion. For example the following sentence is quite understandable:

I enclose copies of the letter and order.

It is obvious from the context that there are two documents—a letter and an order. But what does this next sentence mean?

The filing is done by the secretary and clerk.

It means that there is only one person doing the filing, and that person is both secretary and clerk. If there are two people, you should say 'the secretary and *the* clerk'.

*3. 'Either'*

'Either' refers to one of two things. You can therefore write:

> This carpet comes in beige or green. Either colour would suit the decor you have in mind.

But if there are more than two colours, you should say

> This carpet comes in beige, green and gold. Any one of these colours would suit the decor you have in mind.

## Using adverbs

As their name implies, adverbs qualify verbs—they tell you how, when and where the action was performed. So you can say 'I went there', 'I wrote to you yesterday', 'He spoke well'. 'There', 'yesterday' and 'well' are all adverbs. But adverbs do not *only* qualify verbs. They can qualify other parts of speech as well. In 'very difficult' 'very' qualifies an adjective. In 'just after', 'just' qualifies a preposition. In 'superbly well', 'superbly' qualifies another adverb.

Like adjectives, some adverbs can have comparative and superlative forms. When the adverb consists of only one syllable, like 'soon', it forms the comparative and superlative like an adjective ('sooner', 'soonest'). When it is a long word, and particularly when it ends in -ly, the comparative and superlative are formed by using 'more' and 'most' before the adverb. So the comparative of 'clearly' is 'more clearly', and the superlative is 'most clearly'. Of course, not all adverbs have comparative and superlative forms. You cannot, for example, say 'more very difficult', or 'more just after'.

## Adverbs – potential problems

*1. Correct position of adverb*

Make sure that your positioning of the adverb does not cause confusion, especially when using 'only'. Look at the following sentence:

> I only asked you last week to submit your expenses on the approved form.

As it stands, it means that I only *asked* you last week, I did not order you. What if it was only last week that I asked you—then I should say:

I asked you only last week...

The rule, therefore, is that

- the adverb should go as close as possible to the word it qualifies.

But do not be too dogmatic about it. As long as there is no doubt about the meaning, and as long as the sentence sounds right, it does not matter too much where the adverb goes.

*2. Double adverbs*

When you are using a double adverb, as in 'not only...but also', you must keep the parts of the sentence which follow them 'in parallel'. They must have the same construction. So you should *not* say:

> You have not only failed to supply our order, but also to give a reason for the non-delivery.

'Not only' is followed by the past participle 'failed', while 'but also' is followed by the infinitive 'to give'. For the sentence to be in parallel, they should either *both* be followed by a past participle or *both* by an infinitive. So you should either write

> You have not only failed to supply our order, but also omitted to give a reason for the non-delivery.

*or*

> You have failed not only to supply our order but also to give a reason for the non-delivery.

The same mistake is often made with the double conjunctions 'either...or' and 'neither...nor'.

*3. 'Hardly'*

A common error in writing of all kinds is the one shown in the following sentence:

> I had hardly put the phone down than your parcel arrived.

Can you see what is wrong? 'Hardly' is an adverb expressing time. 'Than' is a conjunction expressing comparison. So the two do not go together. 'Scarcely' and 'hardly' should therefore always be followed by 'when', and the above sentence should read:

> I had hardly put the phone down *when* your parcel arrived.

## PREPOSITIONS

### Explanation

A preposition is a word which shows the relationship of one thing or person to another. 'By', 'to', 'on' 'from', 'with' are all prepositions.

A preposition should always be followed by a noun or pronoun. When it is followed by a pronoun, it should take the **objective** case—'*to* me', '*from* him', '*about* her' etc.

### Potential problems

*1. Do not end with a preposition*

The strict rule is that you should not end a sentence with a preposition. So don't say:

Mrs Graham is the person I spoke to you *about.*

The correct form is:

Mrs Graham is the person *about* whom I spoke to you.

However, you can carry this too far, as in the sentence attributed to Winston Churchill:

This is something *up with* which I will not put.

(He said it deliberately to point out the absurdity of carrying this rule to extremes!)

The sensible thing is to avoid ending a sentence with a preposition if you can, but not if it makes the sentence even clumsier than it was before.

*2. Choosing the correct prepositions*

Certain verbs and adjectives are associated with particular prepositions, and you must use the correct form. Below is a list of those most often used incorrectly, with the correct ones in brackets.

| | |
|---|---|
| accompanied with (by) | oblivious to (of) |
| centre round (on) | opposite from (to) |
| concur with (in) | prevail on (upon) |
| different to or than (from) | replace with (by) |
| distaste of (for) | substitute by (for) |

*3. Words taking more than one preposition*

Some words can take two or more different prepositions, but the meaning changes with the preposition. Be sure that you do not use the wrong preposition, and so give your sentence the wrong meaning. Here are some of the most commonly confused combinations:

agree to (a proposal)
agree with (a person)

concerned at (something that has happened)
concerned for (a person)

correspond with (a person)
correspond to (a thing)

differ from (means 'be different from')
differ with (means 'disagree with')

entrust to (a person)
entrust with (a thing)

impatient with (a person)
impatient of (authority, criticism etc.)

interfere in (a dispute etc)
interfere with (a person)

*4. 'Among' and 'between'*
The preposition 'among' applies only when you are writing about three or more people or things. If you are writing about two, then you should use 'between'. So you can write:

You can divide the territory among the four of you.

But you should say

You can divide the territory *between* the two of you.

## CONJUNCTIONS

### Explanation
Conjunctions are 'connecting' words. They are used to join two or more words, phrases or clauses together. So in the phrase 'you and me', 'and' is a conjunction. There are two kinds of conjunction:

- **co-ordinating** conjunctions, like 'and', 'but', 'yet', 'nor' 'or', which combine words, phrases and clauses of equal weight;

- **subordinating** conjunctions, like 'because', 'therefore', 'before', 'since', 'although', 'unless', which connect a subsidiary clause to the main one.

Let us look at these conjunctions in action, and spot the difference:

> We have looked through our records, but I am afraid that we can find no trace of your order.
>
> I will take no further action unless I hear from you.

In the first sentence, 'we have looked through our records' and 'I am afraid that we can find no trace of your order' are equally important. Neither is dependent on the other. You cannot really say which expresses the main idea of the sentence. In the second sentence, however, 'I hear from you' is dependent on 'I will take no further action' for its relevance. The main idea of the sentence is 'I will take no action'. 'I hear from you' is 'subordinate' to that idea, so it is introduced by a subordinating conjunction.

## Potential problems

*1. 'Either...or'*

'Either...or' and 'neither...nor' should always be followed by a singular verb if they are followed by singular nouns. So it is wrong to say:

> Neither invoice 23765 nor invoice 24534 have been paid.

It should be:

> Neither invoice 23765 nor invoice 24534 *has* been paid.

What it means is that invoice 23765 has not been paid, nor has invoice 24534 been paid. You are simply replacing two verbs with one, so it remains a singular verb. Of course, if the nouns are plural, you use a plural verb. So you would say:

> Neither the sales representatives nor the demonstrators are happy with their pay increases.

*2. Joining clauses*

When choosing a conjunction to join two clauses, think carefully. If you use a co-ordinating conjunction to introduce a subsidiary clause, you will give the clause too much weight. There is a subtle difference between:

> The Managing Director will be at our sales conference this week, and will not be able to give you a reply until next Monday.

and:

> The Managing Director will be at our sales conference this week, and will therefore not be able to give you a reply until next Monday.

In the first sentence, the two clauses are equal. This means that although the ideas are connected, the connection is not particularly close. So the fact that the Managing Director cannot give you a reply may be only partly due to his being at the sales conference. The implication is that there are other factors as well.

In the second sentence, the second clause is very definitely tied to the first by the word 'therefore'. He cannot give you a reply—solely because he will be at the sales conference. So choose your conjunctions with care and do not use a co-ordinating one in a subordinating role.

*3. Unrelated ideas*

Do not use conjunctions to connect unrelated ideas. Do not, for example, say something like:

> We had to make two people redundant this month and sales were up by 50 per cent.

It sounds as though the two events were connected. As we saw in Chapter 4, each sentence should contain a single idea or two related ideas. If the ideas are not related, they should be in separate sentences.

*4. Expressing similarities*

When expressing a similarity, you can use the conjunction 'as' or the preposition 'like', as in 'We need a computer like theirs' or 'We should be compiling our accounts as they compile theirs.' But the two words are not interchangeable. Like all prepositions, the word 'like' can only be used with a noun or pronoun. If the word is to introduce a clause, you should use the conjunction 'as'. So it is wrong to say:

> Why can we not achieve a consistently high quality, like they do?

You should say, '*as* they do' because 'they do' is a clause, not a noun.

*5. Starting a sentence with a conjunction*

Strictly speaking, it is wrong to start a sentence with a conjunction. However, the practice has become so common that it is now quite acceptable, provided that the conjunction is a *co-ordinating* one. You can therefore say:

> We can offer you all the training facilities you might need, including the most-up-to-date audio-visual equipment. And if you have any special requirements, we will do our best to meet them.

But you cannot start a sentence with a *subordinating* conjunction. The reason is that a subordinating conjunction introduces a subordinate clause—one that depends on the main clause for its meaning. If you separate the subordinate clause from the main one, therefore, it loses its meaning. You can see what I mean in the following passage.

> I am afraid that we will not be renewing our contract with you. Because, despite several warnings, you have not provided the level of service we require.

The second part of this passage does not make sense on its own because it is only there to qualify the first part—it explains why you will not be renewing the contract. You must therefore write it as one sentence:

> I am afraid that we will not be renewing our contract with you because, despite several warnings, you have not provided the level of service we require.

## PHRASES AND CLAUSES

### Explanation

Phrases and clauses are groups of words within a sentence. The difference is that a clause contains a subject and a predicate and a phrase does not. For most practical purposes, this difference is of purely academic interest.

There are many different kinds of phrase and clause, but they are really of interest only to grammarians. The main ones we need to be aware of in day-to-day business communication are adjectival and adverbial phrases and clauses—the ones that act as adjectives or adverbs, qualifying other words. For example, consider the following sentences:

> Thank you for your cheque, which arrived today.
> After two weeks without a response, I decided to call on the customer.

In the first sentence, 'which arrived today' is an adjectival clause: it qualifies the noun 'cheque'. It describes the cheque, just as an adjective would. In the second, 'after two weeks without a response' is an adverbial phrase qualifying the verb 'decided'. It describes when I decided, just as an adverb would.

### Potential problems

*1. Adjectival and adverbial phrases and clauses*

The most common error with adjectival and adverbial phrases and clauses is separating them from the words they qualify. Look at the following sentences:

> No one may remove anything from the stationery cupboard except Miss Brown.
>
> We have had to ask you to deliver the new machine four times.

In the first sentence, it sounds as though the only thing you can remove from the cupboard is Miss Brown! The adjectival phrase 'except Miss Brown' should go next to the pronoun it qualifies, 'no one'. So the sentence should read:

> No one except Miss Brown may remove anything from the stationery cupboard.

In the second sentence, it sounds as though we wanted you to deliver the machine four times. The adverbial phrases 'four times' should go next to the verb it qualifies, 'ask'. So the sentence should read:

> We have had to ask you four times to deliver the new machine.

A particularly common variation of this error is the **hanging participle**. The following sentence is an example:

> Arriving at the conference centre, the Manager had left.

The present participle 'arriving', which introduces the adjectival phrase 'arriving at the conference centre' has nothing to qualify, and is left hanging—hence the term hanging participle. It looks as though it qualifies 'the Manager', but that makes the sentence nonsensical. The sentence needs rewriting, so that the phrase has something to qualify. So you would say:

> Arriving at the conference centre, *we found* that the Manager had left.

Now the adjectival phrase has something to qualify—'we'—and the sentence makes sense.

*2. Omitting the second subject*

When two clauses are joined by a conjunction, it is quite common to leave out the subject of the second clause if it is the same as the subject of the first. So you can say

> I hope this clarifies the situation and I look forward to hearing from you

*or*

I hope this clarifies the situation and look forward to hearing from you.

But you should not leave out the second subject if it is different from the first. The following sentence is wrong:

Your queries are being investigated and will be in touch shortly.

This sounds as though 'your queries' will be in touch shortly, which is of course absurd. The reason for the confusion is that the subject of the first clause, 'your queries', is not the same as the subject of the second. The person who will be in touch is you, the writer. So the sentence should read:

Your queries are being investigated and I will be in touch shortly.

## CHECKLIST

- Have you used capital letters only for proper nouns?
- Are all your collective and compound nouns followed by singular verbs?
- Is your use of pronouns ambiguous, or is it clear who or what is referred to?
- Do your relative pronouns relate back to a noun or pronoun?
- Are you clear which is the subject of each verb? Does each verb agree with its subject?
- Have you avoided splitting infinitives?
- Have you used the active voice wherever possible?
- Are your qualifying words and phrases as close to the words they qualify as possible?
- Do you know the difference between the comparative and superlative forms, and have you used them correctly?
- Do you use the right prepositions with the right verbs?
- Are there any hanging participles in your document?

## SUGGESTED EXERCISE

### Correct the grammar of the following passages

1. The Board was asked to carefully consider the Proposal. It was only given conditional approval after a lengthy discussion.

2. On Wednesday, Keith Hamilton had a meeting with Simon Kitson. He said that next week he would be in Paris, where Peterson & Martin have their European Office, so he could

discuss the contract then.

3. We have had a good response to our advertisement for a sales manager, and Henry Johnson would like to discuss the applications with you and I on Tuesday.

4. I do not mind you asking for time off, but it would be nice if I occasionally saw you working late as well. You appear to be getting rather behind with your work. Which is affecting the efficiency of the whole department.

5. You say that you have not had the copy invoices and credit notes you asked for which makes it difficult to reconcile the account. Your accountant and me have had a lengthy correspondence over this matter, and I think you will find that he has a copy of all the relevant documentation.

6. The Committee have decided that every member, together with his or her spouse, have the right to use the facilities of the centre.

7. Having considered all the estimates we received, you will be pleased to know that we have decided to accept yours. None of the other firms were able to match your price or delivery times.

8. Please can you see to it that every secretary and typist, including the directors' personal assistants, are made aware of this new house style. We must not only ensure that we create a good image but also a consistent one.

9. David Smith & Co has been taken over by the Robertson Corporation. When the Board heard the news, they were in disagreement over what action to take, which meant that a decision was deferred.

# 8
# Punctuating Correctly

In order to make your communication clear and easy to read, you need to punctuate it. Punctuation marks indicate **pauses** in a sentence, and you need to strike a balance between too many and too few of them. If you have too many, your document is broken up too much and becomes disjointed. If you have too few, it becomes difficult to follow. The following passage has no punctuation marks at all. Can you see how difficult it is to see what the writer means?

> I am afraid that owing to the fact that the Managing Director is out of the office at the moment it is not possible to agree to your request immediately not that it is likely to be turned down of course but we do need his approval for agreements of this nature however he will be back next week and I will make sure that he deals with it as soon as possible.

Now here is the same passage, but overpunctuated:

> I am afraid that, owing to the fact, that the Managing Director is out of the office, at the moment, it is not possible to agree to your request, immediately—not that it is likely to be turned down, of course; but we do need his approval, for agreements of this nature. However, he will be back next week; and I will make sure that he deals with it, as soon as possible.

Can you see how disjointed it is to read?—almost jerky in fact. Let us see how it looks when properly punctuated:

> I am afraid that, owing to the fact that the Managing Director is out of the office at the moment, it is not possible to agree to your request immediately—not that it is likely to be turned down of course, but we do need his approval for agreements of this nature. However, he will be back next week and I will make sure that he deals with it as soon as possible.

This is easier to read than the other two versions, and the sense is quite clear the first time you read it.

## THE FOUR MAIN PURPOSES OF PUNCTUATION

Punctuation serves four main purposes.

*To divide things up*
It **divides** what you are writing into easily absorbed parts—sentences, clauses, phrases etc. The following sentence shows this:

> I am enclosing our latest catalogue, in which you will find all our current models.

The comma breaks the sentence into two parts, which are easier to read than one long one.

*To indicate a relationship*
It indicates the **relationship** between parts of a sentence, as in the following sentence:

> The catalogue (which has just been published) contains details of our current models.

The brackets indicate that the clause they enclose is an aside—it is not part of the main theme of the sentence.

*To differentiate meanings*
It can be used to **differentiate between two meanings** of the same sentence. For example:

> Sales are up by 15 per cent more than we budgeted for

has a different meaning from

> Sales are up by 15 per cent—more than we budgeted for.

*To emphasise*
It can emphasise certain words or phrases, as in

> There is only one possible outcome in this situation—bankruptcy.

Using the dash in this way emphasises the word 'bankruptcy'.

Punctuation is often a matter of style, but there are certain rules which should be followed if your correspondence is to make sense to your readers. In this chapter, we will be looking at both the rules and the points of style governing punctuation marks.

## FULL STOPS

The rules for using full stops are probably the simplest and most widely understood of all punctuation marks. There are just two occasions when a full stop is used:

- to end a sentence, as in:

  Mr Graham has passed your letter on to me.

- after initials or abbreviations, as in 'P.J. Darwin', 'Inc.', 'Co.' (but note that a full stop is not necessary after a contraction—an abbreviation in which the first and last letters are the same as in the full word, like Dr, Mr, St, Ltd)

## COMMAS

The rules governing commas are not quite so straightforward as those for full stops. That is because they are the most flexible of all punctuation marks, and where you use them is to a large extent a matter of taste. The basic guidelines for using commas are as follows:

### To separate words or phrases in a list

For example:

> We can offer a choice of beige, black, dark blue or grey trim.

Note that when you use commas in this way, it is not usual to have one before the final 'or' or 'and'—only put one in if it is necessary for the sake of clarity.

You can use a comma to separate adjectives qualifying the same noun, as in:

> Please enclose a large, brown envelope.

This again is a matter of preference, and you could just as well leave the comma out. One situation in which you *must* leave it out is when the second adjective and the noun actually form a compound noun together. Take 'filing cabinet' as an example. 'Filing' is not a qualifying adjective in this context. It is part of the noun. A filing cabinet is something very different from an ordinary cabinet, so 'filing' does not describe the cabinet in the way that 'brown' describes the envelope in the previous example. So you should not write

> Please supply a large, filing cabinet.

**To join two clauses**

When two clauses are joined by a co-ordinating conjunction, you can use a comma or not. So you would write:

> I strongly disagree and I think you should reconsider.

*or*

> I strongly disagree, and I think you should reconsider.

Whether or not you use a comma in this context will depend on your own preference, the length of the sentence and the amount of separation you want to show. So if your sentence is long you might put in a comma, introducing a pause so that the reader can absorb what he or she has read so far. If the ideas in the clauses are not closely related, you might put in a comma to increase the impression of separation. If, on the other hand, they are closely related, you might leave the comma out so as to bring them closer in the reader's mind.

**To separate an introductory signal**

You can use a comma to separate the introductory signalling word in a sentence from the rest. For example:

> Finally, may I offer my congratulations on your success this year.

**To create parentheses**

You can use commas as parentheses, when you insert something which either expands on the main sentence without affecting its meaning or qualifies part of it. For example:

> This is not, I am sure, what the Board had in mind.

> Mr Jones, the Senior Partner, will be in touch shortly.

In both these cases, the main part of the sentence stands perfectly well on its own, without the section in parenthesis. For other kinds of parentheses, see **Brackets** and **Dashes** below.

### To introduce direct speech

You must use either a comma or a colon to introduce direct speech or a quotation of a full sentence from another source, as in:

> Jonathan Wallace's report says, 'We must encourage our employees to participate fully in the decisions which govern their working lives.'

If you are only quoting a few words, then you need not introduce the quotation with a comma. So you can say:

> Jonathan Wallace's report says that we should encourage our employees to participate fully in 'the decisions which govern their working lives'.

In this case only the last part of the clause is a direct quotation, so no comma is used to introduce it.

### To separate for easier reading

Commas can be used to separate phrases and clauses if necessary to make your document easier to read, as in

> Since you have not replied to my letter, I assume that you agree with my suggestion.
>
> Reading your report, I was struck by its clarity.

### To avoid confusion

Commas can be useful to avoid confusion, even in situations where you would not normally use them. Look at the following sentence:

> The outfits are available in red and white and brown and beige.

Are the outfits available in four colours or in two combinations of two colours each? It is not clear. To make your meaning absolutely clear, it would be better to write:

> The outfits are available in red and white, and brown and beige.

Although the use of commas is largely a matter of taste and style, you should not overuse them. If you do your document will have too many pauses in it, and will become disjointed. Look at the following sentence:

> However, if we invest in new plant, and the market falls again, as it could easily do, we might, conceivably, find ourselves with too much production capacity, which could, perhaps, cause even graver problems.

None of these commas is actually wrong, but there are just too many of them. We are forced to read the sentence in jerks. You need to use your discretion and cut out a few inessential ones so that the sentence flows.

## SEMICOLONS

The semicolon is probably the most undervalued of all punctuation marks; it can be extremely useful yet it is very seldom used. Like the comma, its use is very much a matter of personal preference and style. Basically it is used to indicate a longer pause than a comma would give, but shorter than a full stop. There are four situations for which the semicolon is useful.

### To separate clearly

It can be used to separate statements which are closely connected, but not so closely as to justify either a comma or a conjunction. For example:

> I like your proposal; it is well thought out and workable.

The two ideas are connected, so it would look wrong if they were two separate sentences. On the other hand

> I like your proposal because it is well thought out and workable

ties the two ideas too closely together. It sounds as though you like the proposal *only* because it is well thought out and workable.

### To emphasise a statement

It can be used to emphasise a statement, or to make it more punchy. As you can see if you read the above example again, almost any statement after the semicolon is given extra emphasis. Here is another example.

> We must improve our productivity; we face bankruptcy if we do not.

The second part of this sentence stands out starkly—far more so than if it had been written

> We must improve our productivity because we face bankruptcy if we do not.

### To convey contrasts

It can be used to balance contrasting statements, as in

> We offer a home delivery service; other firms do not.

As in the above examples, the emphasis is on the second statement, but the main purpose of the semicolon here is to highlight the contrast between your service and that of other firms.

### To separate longer items in a list

We saw under **Commas** above that commas are also used to separate items in a list. There is no absolute rule to say when you should use commas and when you should use semicolons, but a good rule of thumb is that semicolons should be used when the items in the list are clauses and when the items themselves contain commas. Let us look at some examples.

> I recommend the following: that we increase our sales staff by five; that we double our advertising budget; and that we introduce more stringent quality control measures.

> We have three main requirements: high-quality, durable materials; reasonable prices; and fast, reliable delivery.

In the first example, the items in the list are clauses; to separate them only with commas would make them appear to run into each other. In the second, there are commas in two of the items in the list. If the items themselves were separated by commas, it would be confusing to read. Unlike commas, when you are using semicolons to separate items in a list, you *do* have a semicolon before the final 'and' or 'or'.

## COLONS

The colon has only three uses.

- It is used to **introduce lists**, as in

  I would be grateful if you would let me have your cheque for the following invoices which are overdue: No 14352 of 6 January, No 21345 of 29 January and No 25431 of 14 February.

- It can be used to indicate two sides of the same theme; the first part of the sentence makes a statement, and the second part explains it. For example:

  The solution is simple: train more operators.
  The reasons are the same in both cases: we are undervaluing our key staff.

- It can be used instead of a comma to introduce direct speech or a quotation.

## BRACKETS

There are two kinds of brackets:

- round brackets (called **parentheses**) which are the brackets we are all familiar with, namely these: ( )

- square brackets, which look like this: [ ]

Each serves a different purpose, and they should not be confused.

### Parentheses

Using parentheses is a bit like saying 'By the way' in speech. They are used for asides, for indicating that a passage is not part of the main theme of the sentence, but is added by way of explanation or comment. So you might write

> There is still £1,235 outstanding on your account (see enclosed statement).

The part in brackets is an extension of the main part of the sentence, but it does not express part of the sentence's idea. It is therefore an aside.

Beware of using brackets for very long passages. They break up the sentence and cause the reader to pause; if the pause is too long, the reader will lose track of what the sentence is about. Consider the following sentence:

> Susan King (who was appointed Managing Director on the resignation of Martin Wilson in January) will be addressing the conference next week.

The passage in brackets is so long that by the time it ends, the reader can hardly remember what the subject of the sentence is. Anything that long is seldom likely to be a real aside. As a rule of thumb, you should not use brackets for adjectival phrases or clauses. You should enclose them in commas instead. So the above sentence would be better written as

> Susan King, who was appointed Managing Director on the resignation of Martin Wilson in January, will be addressing the conference next week.

The commas do not separate the passage from the rest of the sentence to the same extent as brackets, and the whole thing reads more smoothly.

This leads us on to a second rule of thumb. If you want to put a passage in parenthesis, but do not know whether to use commas, brackets or dashes, remember that commas denote less of a pause than brackets, which denote less of a pause than dashes. So you can choose your punctuation marks according to how much separation you want. Commas will connect the passage closely to the rest of the sentence, brackets less closely, and dashes will separate it out most of all.

Brackets can also be used to enclosed explanations of terms or abbreviations or to show reference sources. It is normal practice to explain an abbreviation only once, the first time you use it. So you might write:

> There are no reliable statistics on the country's GNP (Gross National Product), and this makes planning difficult. However, as a guide international experts estimate that its GNP is among the ten lowest in the world.

If you are writing a report and referring to, or quoting from, someone else's work, it is only right that you should acknowledge their contribution. This is often done by putting your source in brackets after you have referred to it, as in:

> A leading human resources management expert believes that all managerial personnel ought to be retrained in the techniques of managing change (H.K. Barton, *Human Resources Management in a Changing Environment*).

If you have an acknowledgements section in your report, and the full title of the book, article, report or leaflet you are referring to is shown in that section, then you might just show the author (and possibly the page on which the reference appears).

### Square brackets

You will not often need to use square brackets, but it is as well to know how their use differs from round ones.

Square brackets are used when you are quoting directly from another source, and you want to add something of your own—usually an expansion. The following passage shows an example:

> Suresh Desai's report states:
>
> 'If we wish to improve our image, then we must ensure that they [the customers] are treated not only courteously but also in a friendly and helpful way.'

This indicates that *you* have inserted 'the customers' to explain who 'they' refer to.

## DASHES

However and wherever you use them dashes increase the emphasis of what you are saying. The part of the sentence after the dash—or between the dashes in the case of two dashes—will always carry more emphasis than without the dash. Dashes have four main functions.

- You can use two dashes to put something in parenthesis. They are more abrupt and emphatic than brackets, and they provide a greater separation between the passage in parenthesis and the rest of the sentence. Here is an example:

  Your inability to deliver our components on time has cost us a great deal—in time, in manpower and in lost sales—and we feel that a full explanation of the delay is called for.

- Two dashes can also be used to pull together or summarise several items, as in

  Word processors, filing cabinets, bookshelves, filing trays—in fact all office equipment—should be listed.

- One dash can be used to sum up or comment on what has gone before in an emphatic way, as in

  You did not pay within the specified time, so we stopped your account—as is normal business practice.

- One dash can also be used to denote a sudden change of thought, or a new, but connected idea, as in

  Please do not smoke in the office—or at least confine it to the toilets.

## APOSTROPHES

The apostrophe has three uses.

- It is used to show that a letter or letters have been **left out** of a word, as in 'don't' for 'do not', 'we'll' for 'we will' or 'let's' for 'let us'.

- It is often used when writing the **plural** of a **letter**, as in

  We must ensure that all the i's are dotted and all the t's crossed.

- It is used to denote the **possessive** form of a noun, as in 'Peter's letter' or 'the clients' files'. Note that when it is used to denote the possessive of a plural noun ending in 's', the apostrophe comes after the 's'. If you are using it with a singular noun, or a plural noun which does *not* end in 's', then the apostrophe comes before the 's'. So you would write 'the customer's account' but 'the customers' accounts', 'ladies' clothes' but 'women's clothes'.

  There is a tendency today to leave the apostrophe out when writing the possessive, particularly in posters or signs. So you will often see a sign saying 'Ladies Wear' or 'Mens Hairdresser'. Do not be tempted to follow suit. There may come a time when it will be acceptable to omit the apostrophe, but it has not arrived yet. Although some of your correspondents will accept it, many will see it as a sign of carelessness or ignorance.

  Many people have trouble with possessives of names that end in 's'. Should they, for example, write 'Mr Jones's order' or 'Mr Jones' order'? The answer is that there is no hard and fast rule, and either is acceptable.

  Two words which constantly cause problems are 'its' and 'it's'. when should you use an apostrophe, and when not? When it is short for 'it is', then you should use an apostrophe—'it's'. When it means 'belonging to it', do not use an apostrophe—'its'.

## QUOTATION MARKS

Often called **inverted commas**, quotation marks are used for quotations, as their name implies. There are four occasions when you should use them.

- For **direct speech**, as in

  He said, 'I cannot agree with your proposal.'

  You will seldom use direct speech in business documents, so you are not likely to come across this usage.

- When **quoting** the exact words of a person, document, book or article, as in

  Norman Tipton wrote of a 'potentially damaging recession' looming.

- for **irony**, as in

  What you do think of Green & Co's 'new' corporate image?

  The implication behind this use is that you do not believe that Green & Co's corporate image is actually very new.

- To indicate claims or points made by someone else which you do not want to form part of your own argument, as in

  Smiths have developed a new 'quick-dry' paint.

  This means that Smiths are claiming it is quick to dry. You are not necessarily denying the claim, but nor are you confirming it. You may not have enough information to form a judgement. Or it could simply be that whether it is quick to dry or not makes no difference to your own argument—perhaps it is the claim itself that is important.

Whether you use single ( ' ) or double quotation marks ( " ) is a matter of personal preference. It is usual these days to use single ones, except perhaps for direct speech, but if you prefer double then use them.

Very occasionally you may need to write a **quote within a quote**. If you are using single quotation marks, then the quote within a quote should be in double marks, and vice versa. So you might write:

> Kendall says, 'The provision of unnecessary "executive" gimmicks for management is proving costly.'

*or*

Kendall says, "The provision of unnecessary 'executive' gimmicks for management is proving costly."

## EXCLAMATION MARKS

Exclamation marks are seldom necessary or advisable in business correspondence. As their name implies, they indicate an exclamation, and you should be reasoning and persuading in your writing, not exclaiming.

Some people use exclamation marks to provide emphasis. This is incorrect and looks amateurish. So do not write

We can offer you the best bargains ever!

You should be able to provide all the emphasis you need by your choice of words, and by the use of other punctuation marks.

There is one situation in which it is quite legitimate to use the exclamation mark in business correspondence, and that is in a semi-humorous context, or to denote irony, as in

Somebody has been posting letters in the litter bin!

The suggestion is 'What a silly thing to do.'

## QUESTION MARKS

There is only one rule for using question marks. They end sentences which are questions, as in

Could we meet on Tuesday to discuss your report in detail?

However, you can also use them in informal documents, especially internal memos, as a sort of shorthand. You might, for example, write

We must meet (? Friday) to discuss the arrangements.

This means 'We must meet to discuss the arrangements. Would Friday suit you?' I must emphasise, however, that it is an informal device, and should only be used in internal and informal communications.

## HYPHENS

The hyphen is a very useful device, particularly in avoiding confusing or awkward constructions. It is used in the following ways:

- To connect two or more words to form a **compound word**, especially a compound adjective, as in ‘a ground-floor office’, ‘a like-minded colleague’ or ‘a sales-generating strategy’. However, you should not use a hyphen to make a compound adjective when the first word is an adverb ending in -ly. So you should write ‘a well-designed product’, but ‘a beautifully designed product’.

- To connect two words to make a **compound noun**, as in ‘car-park’. If you are unsure whether a compound noun is written as one word, hyphenated or two words (and it is not always easy to know), check your dictionary.

- To differentiate between words beginning with **re-** which are spelt the same but have different meanings. So you would write ‘reform’, meaning ‘improve’ but ‘re-form’, meaning ‘form again’, ‘recount’ meaning ‘tell’, but ‘re-count’ meaning ‘count again’.
- To **connect a letter** to a noun to form a compound, as in ‘T-junction’ or ‘U-turn’.

- To make a **compound number**, as in ‘twenty-eight’.

- To avoid an **awkward repetition** of a letter, as in ‘co-operate’, ‘anti-inflation’.

- To **differentiate** between two possible meanings of the same passage. So you could have ‘a grey flecked carpet’ (a grey carpet with flecks) or a ‘grey-flecked carpet’ (a carpet with grey flecks). Or you could have ‘a country sports-club’ (a sports club in the country) or ‘a country-sports club’ (a club for country sports).

## CHECKLIST

- Which abbreviations take a full stop, and which do not?
- Have you got enough commas to help your readers make sense of your document, without having so many that they interfere with the flow of your sentence?
- Can you see which parenthetical passages need commas, which need brackets and which need dashes?

- Have you used semicolons or dashes to provide emphasis?
- If you have a list, have you chosen the right punctuation marks to separate the items?
- Can you distinguish between passages which need round brackets and those which need square ones?
- Have you used apostrophes for your possessives? Are they in the right place?

## SUGGESTED EXERCISE

**Punctuate the following passages.**

1. The Managing Director who is abroad at present has asked me to reply to your letter concerning the contract for the new equipment although we agree with the terms in general there are a few points that we would like explained

2. Our new catalogue enclosed contains details of all our latest lines in particular you may be interested in the following the Newline typists desk the updated ergonomically designed Comfort swivel chair and the Locksafe filing system

3. We have five different models each with its own special features and they all come in a choice of three finishes so whatever your needs you will find one to suit you
4. The expansion of our business is a long term project and we need an efficient sympathetic management consultant to help us a recent report said any small business hoping to expand will find its chance of success greatly improved by the employment of a consultant to advise it we would I think be foolish to embark on this exercise without outside help

5. We are very concerned about your payment record your payments are invariably two months late at the moment we are awaiting payment of Invoices 14325 16754 and 23156 all of which are well overdue

# 9
# Spelling and Vocabulary

English is derived from a number of different sources—Norman, Anglo-Saxon, Latin, Viking—with Arab, Indian, French, African and other influences. So the rules of spelling are not always easy. There are moreover a number of words which have similar spellings but very different meanings. All of this can make it difficult to use just the right word, and to spell it correctly, every time. You should therefore have a good dictionary handy and *always* refer to it if you are unsure about a word's spelling, or about its precise meaning and usage. If it is only the spelling you are concerned about, there are some excellent little spelling dictionaries available.

No book can hope to cover every word which is likely to cause difficulty; different words cause problems for different people. This chapter will therefore only cover the words which are most commonly used or spelt incorrectly. If there are others with which you regularly have difficulty, then it is a good idea to make a list of them, so that you can refer to it every time you want to use a particular word. You will soon learn the correct spelling or usage.

## COMMONLY MISSPELT WORDS

The following points cover the most common spelling errors found in business correspondence.

### Prefixes

When prefixes like dis-, un- or mis- are attached to words which begin with the same consonant as the prefix ending, the letter is doubled. So you have

dissolve, not disolve
unnatural, not unatural
misspell, not mispell

## American spellings

Some people, particularly in the business field, seem to prefer to use American spellings, as though they somehow enhance their image as go-ahead business people. American spellings are not yet accepted in Britain, and may well never be. If you use them you will not appear go-ahead. You will appear either careless or ignorant. So use

| | |
|---|---|
| honour | not honor |
| colour | not color |
| favourite | not favorite |
| centre | not center |
| travelled | not traveled |
| licence | not license (as a noun—see below) |
| programme | not program, except a computer program which is spelt the American way, even in British English. |

## The final 'l'

As you can see from the above, British English forms the past tense of 'travel' by doubling the 'l', whereas American English does not. The rule for forming both the -ed and the -ing forms of verbs ending in 'l' (and nouns from them) is that you double the 'l' if there is only one vowel before it, and not if there are two. So you would write traveller, appalling, controlled, but dealer, appealing, pooled.

## Adverbs

Adverbs formed from adjectives usually just add -ly to the adjective, as in quickly, recently, slowly. If the adjective ends in -ic, however, the adverb is formed by adding -ally. So you would write:

basically not basicly
radically not radicly
stoically not stoicly

There is just one exception to this rule. 'Public' becomes 'publicly', not 'publically'.

## 'C' and 's'

There are some words which have slightly different spellings, depending on whether they are used as verbs or nouns. Be sure that you know the difference. They are

| | |
|---|---|
| licence (noun) | license (verb) |
| practice (noun) | practise (verb) |
| advice (noun) | advise (verb) |

The best way to remember which spelling to use for each form is to think of 'advise'. Here the pronunciation changes as well, as you can hear as soon as you say the word that the -ise form is the verb and the -ice form is the noun. The others follow the same pattern.

### More common spelling traps

- A very common error is to write 'alright'. The correct form is 'all right'.
- Do not confuse 'dependant' and 'dependent'. A dependant is a person who is dependent on someone else.
- Other commonly misspelt words are:

| | | |
|---|---|---|
| accumulate | eighth | parallel |
| acquire | embarrass | questionnaire |
| across | exaggerate | schedule |
| appreciate | fascinate | seize |
| chaotic | feasible | successful |
| commemorate | imminent | supersede |
| commission | instalment | tariff |
| concede | issuing | thorough |
| conceivable | liaison | unmistakable |
| conscientious | manoeuvre | |
| deferred | occasion | |

## COMMONLY CONFUSED WORDS

Confusion often arises between words which sound similar but are spelt slightly differently, and between words which have slightly different shades of meaning. As I have said, this section is not intended to provide a comprehensive list of these words, only to indicate the ones that cause most confusion.

### Anti- and ante-

A great deal of confusion arises from the prefixes anti- and ante-. Anti- means 'against', ante- means 'before'. So

antisocial means 'against society'
anticlimax means 'against a climax' (i.e. the opposite of a climax)
antedate means 'date before' something
antecedent means 'going before'

### For- and fore-

Similar confusion arises from the prefixes for- and fore-. For- means 'not' or 'against', fore- means 'before'. So

forbid means 'bid not to'
forswear means 'swear not to'
forgoing means 'going not' (i.e. going without)
forerunner means 'something or someone who runs before'
foretell means 'tell before' (i.e. tell before it happens)
foregoing means 'going before'

### Less and fewer

'Less' and 'fewer' cause problems. 'Less' is used for quantity, 'fewer' for number. So you can have less work, less confusion, less chance of promotion, but fewer employees, fewer problems, fewer chances of promotion.

### Infer and imply

A common mistake is to use 'infer' when you mean 'imply'. 'Imply' means to hint at something, as in

> He implied that his company would be receptive to an approach from us.

'Infer' means to gain an impression or draw a conclusion, as in

> I inferred from what he said that his company would be receptive to an approach from us.

So you could say that you infer what someone else has implied.

### 'Alternative'

'Alternative' means one of two choices. It follows that if there are three or more options open to you, you cannot have an alternative—the word to use then is 'choice'or 'option'. So you can say

> There are two alternatives. We can either credit your account or replace the goods.

But you would say

> There are three options. You can return the goods for full credit, we can replace them or we can offer you an extra discount to compensate you.

## Affect and effect

'Affect' and 'effect' are particularly confusing. 'Affect' is a verb, as in

> The fall in productivity will inevitably affect our profitability.

'Effect' is the noun derived from 'affect', as in

> The fall in productivity will inevitably have an effect on our profitability.

However, confusion arises because 'effect' can also be a verb, meaning 'bring about'. So if you were to say

> The fall in productivity will inevitably effect our profitability

you would be saying that the fall will *bring about* your profitability, which is not the same thing at all!

## Confused pairs of words

The following are some of the most commonly confused pairs of words, with their different meanings:

*alternate* (every second one)
I can work alternate Saturdays.

*alternative* (one of two possible options)
An alternative strategy would be...

*biannual* (twice a year)

*biennial* (every two years)

*complement* (go well with or complete)
This line of business would complement our present activities.

*compliment* (praise)
I must compliment you on an excellent report.

*continual* (frequent and repeated)
We must try to avoid these continual absences.

*continuous* (without stop)
We hope to achieve continuous production by next month.

*definite* (not vague)
We need a definite answer by tomorrow.

*definitive* (final or authoritative)
This is the definitive version of the production manual.

*disinterested* (with no vested interest)
If there is any dispute I would suggest that we appeal to a disinterested party to resolve it.

*uninterested* (not interested)
The Chairman is totally uninterested in the day-to-day running of the company.

*enquiry* (question)
Thank you for your enquiry about our service.

*inquiry* (investigation)
I have asked our Distribution Manager to conduct a full inquiry into the reasons for the delay.

*ensure* (make sure)
I would be grateful if you could ensure that we are credited with the full amount.

*insure* (take out insurance)
I trust that the goods are insured against damage in transit.

*meter* (something which measures)
I understand that the error arose as a result of a faulty meter.

*metre* (a unit of measurement)
The fabric comes in metre lengths.

*practical* (concerned with practice, not theory)
At this stage we should be looking at practical steps to implement the decisions we have made.

*practicable* (able to be put into practice)
The programme you have outlined is hardly practicable in the time allowed.

*precede* (go before)
The decision to close the depot preceded the announcement of the year's profits.

*proceed* (begin or go ahead)
We shall proceed with the new arrangements as soon as we have your agreement.

*principal* (main)
My principal objection to your proposal is the cost involved.

*principle* (fundamental belief or truth)
The principles of efficient business practice are the same, whether one is dealing with a one-person business or a multinational corporation.

*stationary* (standing still)
Our van was stationary when your lorry hit it.

*stationery* (writing materials)
I would like to order the following items of stationery.

If you can differentiate between these words in your writing, then you will avoid most of the confusion that commonly arises in business communication. But do remember that these lists and the points raised are not exhaustive. Make friends with your dictionary, and consult it whenever you have any doubts at all.

## CHECKLIST

- Have you checked in your dictionary for any words whose spelling or usage you are unsure of?
- Have you got a list of the words that cause *you* most difficulty?
- What is the difference between 'forgoing' and 'foregoing'?
- Have you used any American spellings?
- Do you know the difference between 'imply' and 'infer'?
- Have you used any words that are spelt similarly to the word you want, but have a different meaning?

# Further Reading

Your first priority should be a good dictionary. The best are published by Collins, Oxford University Press, Chambers and Longmans. They come in a variety of sizes, from pocket editions to large two-volume tomes. Choose one that suits your needs and your budget.

Other books you might like to have or refer to are:

*The Complete Plain Words*, 2nd edition, Sir Ernest Gowers (Penguin 1987). An excellent guide to using plain English and avoiding jargon.

*Dictionary of Modern English Usage*, 2nd edition, H. W. Fowler, revised by Sir Ernest Gowers (Oxford University Press 1965). The 'bible' of English usage.

*Mind the Stop*, G. V. Carey (Penguin 1971). A comprehensive guide to punctuation.

*The Oxford Dictionary for Writers and Editors* (Oxford University Press 1981). An invaluable guide, showing how to spell unusual or difficult words, when to hyphenate words, and a great deal more.

*Titles and Forms of Address—A Guide to Their Correct Use*, 19th edition (A. & C. Black 1990). A complete guide to how to address people, from the Queen to the local vicar.

# Glossary

**Adjective**. A word which qualifies a noun, e.g. little, brown, round.

**Adverb**. A word which qualifies a verb, adjective, preposition or other adverb, e.g. well, clearly, very.

**AIDA**. A formula for remembering the order for an advertisement or sales letter. Stands for Attention, Interest, Desire, Action.

**Ampersand**. The symbol &. An abbreviation for 'and'.

**Appendix**. A section of a report or book which usually gives full details of matters not discussed in detail in the report or book itself.

**Bar chart**. A method of presenting figures visually. Particularly useful for comparing two or more sets of figures at a particular moment.

**bcc**. Typed on copies of a document to indicate that a copy has gone to the person named. A 'blind copy'. Used instead of cc when you do not want the letter's addressee to know that you are sending a copy to a third party.

**Blocked layout**. A layout for a letter in which all lines are ranged left, with no indents.

**cc**. Typed on a document to indicate that a copy is being sent to the person named.

**Charting**. A method of writing an outline for a document, involving making a chart of ideas you want to express.

**Circumlocution**. A phrase or clause which uses more words than are necessary to express an idea.

**Clause**. A group of words within a sentence which has a subject and a predicate.

**Cliché**. A phrase which has been used so often that it has become hackneyed.

**Colloquialism**. A word or expression which is common in speech, but is not acceptable in written English.

**Complex sentence**. A sentence containing a main clause and one or more subordinate clauses.

**Complimentary close**. The ending of a letter. Usually 'Yours sincerely' or 'Yours faithfully' in business correspondence.

**Compound sentence**. A sentence containing two or more clauses joined by a co-ordinating conjunction.

**Compound-complex sentence**. A sentence containing two or more main clauses and one or more subordinate clauses.

**Conjunction**. A word which joins two clauses to form a sentence, eg and, but, however.

**Co-ordinating conjunction**. A conjunction which joins two clauses of equal weight.

**Deduction**. Reasoning from one premise to another to reach a conclusion.

**Edit**. To check a piece of writing for spelling, grammatical and stylistic errors.

**Emotional buying trigger**. An appeal to an emotion or instinct in selling or advertising.

**Enc**. Typed at the bottom of a letter to indicate that something is enclosed.

**Four Ps**. A formula for remembering how to write a sales letter. Stands for Promise, Picture, Proof, Push.

**Freewriting**. A method of writing an outline, involving writing freely as ideas occur to you.

**Full punctuation**. Having all punctuation marks shown, in the inside address, salutation and complimentary close as well as the body of the letter.

**Fully displayed layout**. A layout for a letter in which paragraphs are indented and the date is usually typed on the right-hand side.

**fyi**. For your information. Typed on copies of correspondence sent to a third party to indicate that no action is expected.

**Gerund**. A verbal noun, e.g. writing, coming, reporting.

**Graph**. A method of presenting figures visually. Particularly useful to show a trend over time.

**Hanging participle**. A participle which introduces an adjectival phrase with no noun to qualify.

**Indented layout**. See 'Fully displayed layout'.

**Indexing**. A method of standardising the presentation of figures so that different fields can be compared. It usually involves giving the figures for Year 1 a value of 100, and relating subsequent years' figures to that.

**Induction**. Reaching a conclusion from one's own experience or observation.

**Inside address**. The name and address of the person to whom you are writing, which appears at the top of a letter.

**Jargon**. Language which is specific to a particular group or profession.

**Listing**. A method of writing an outline for a document, involving listing all the points you want to make.

**Logo**. A distinctive device or form of lettering which identifies a company or organisation.

**Noun**. A word which is used to name a person, place or thing, e.g. letter, Harriet Cornish, London.

**Object**. The person or thing which has the action of a sentence done to it. Must be a noun or pronoun.

**Open punctuation**. Having punctuation marks in the body of the letter, but not in the inside address, salutation or complimentary close.

**Parentheses**. Round brackets.

**Phrase**. A group of words within a sentence which does not have a subject and a predicate.

**Pie chart**. A method of showing figures visually. Particularly useful for showing the segmentation of a total figure.

**pp**. Typed or written by your signature when you are signing a letter on behalf of someone else.

**Predicate**. The part of a sentence which describes what the subject did or was. Must contain a verb.

**Preposition**. A word which describes the relationship of one person or thing to another, e.g. by, from, for.

**Pronoun**. A word used instead of a noun, e.g. she, him, your.

**Salutation**. The opening of a letter. Usually begins 'Dear...'

**Semi-blocked layout**. A layout for a letter. Like a blocked layout, but with the date on the right-hand side.

**Sentence**. A group of words complete in itself. Must contain a subject and a predicate.

**Simple sentence**. A sentence containing only one clause.

**Subject**. The person or thing that a sentence is about. Must be either a noun or a pronoun.

**Subordinate clause**. A clause which is dependent on the rest of the sentence for its meaning or relevance.

**Subordinating conjunction**. A conjunction joining a subordinate clause to the rest of the sentence.

**Tautology**. Saying the same thing twice in different words.

**Topic sentence**. A sentence which indicates the topic of a paragraph.

**Unique selling proposition**. Something which makes a product or service unique.

**Vague qualifier**. An adjective or adverb which adds nothing to a description.

**Verb**. A word which describes what is done by or what happens to the subject of a sentence, e.g. agree, have written, will decide.

# Answers to Exercises

Chapter 7

1. The Board was asked to consider the proposal carefully. It was given conditional approval only after a lengthy discussion.
2. On Wednesday, Keith Hamilton had a meeting with Simon Kitson. Keith said that next week he would be in Paris, where Peterson & Martin has its European office, so he could discuss the contract then.
3. We have had a good response to our advertisement for a sales manager, and Henry Johnson would like to discuss the applications with you and me on Tuesday.
4. I do not mind your asking for time off, but it would be nice if I occasionally saw you working late as well. You appear to be getting rather behind with your work, and this is affecting the efficiency of the whole department.
5. You say that you have not had the copy invoices and credit notes you asked for, and that it is therefore difficult to reconcile the account. Your accountant and I have had a lengthy correspondence over this matter, and I think you will find that he has copies of all the relevant documentation.
6. The Committee has decided that every member, together with his or her spouse, has the right to use the facilities of the centre.
7. We have considered all the estimates we received, and you will be pleased to know that we have decided to accept yours. None of the other firms was able to match your price or delivery times.
8. Please can you see to it that every secretary and typist, including the directors' personal assistants, is made aware of this new house style. We must ensure that we create not only a good image but also a consistent one.

9. David Smith & Co has been taken over by the Robertson Corporation. When the Board heard the news, they were in disagreement over what action to take. Because of this, a decision was deferred.

Chapter 9

Because punctuation is to a certain extent a matter of personal taste, there are different ways of punctuating any passage. However, these are the suggested answers:

1. The Managing Director, who is abroad at present, has asked to me to reply to your letter concerning the contract for the new equipment. Although we agree with the terms in general, there are a few points that we would like explained.
2. Our new catalogue (enclosed) contains details of all our latest lines. In particular you may be interested in the following: the Newline typist's desk; the updated, ergonomically designed Comfort swivel chair; and the Locksafe filing system.
3. We have five different models—each with its own special features—and they all come in a choice of three finishes. So whatever your needs, you will find one to suit you.
4. The expansion of our business is a long-term project and we need an efficient, sympathetic management consultant to help us. A recent report, said, 'Any small business hoping to expand will find its chances of success greatly improved by the employment of a consultant to advise it.' We would, I think, be foolish to embark on this exercise without outside help.
5. We are very concerned about your payment record; your payments are invariably two months late. At the moment we are awaiting payment of Invoices 14325, 16754 and 23156, all of which are well overdue.

# Index